NDIC PRESS
NATIONAL DEFENSE INTELLIGENCE COLLEGE

Democratization
of Intelligence

Melding Strategic Intelligence and National Discourse

Russell G. Swenson
and
Susana C. Lemozy
Editors

NATIONAL DEFENSE INTELLIGENCE COLLEGE
WASHINGTON, DC

July 2009

NDIC PRESS

The National Defense Intelligence College supports and encourages research on intelligence issues that distills lessons and improves Intelligence Community capabilities for policy-level and operational consumers.

Democratization of Intelligence: Melding Strategic Intelligence and National Discourse — Russell G. Swenson and Susana C. Lemozy, editors

This abbreviated English edition of the book *Democratización de la Función de Inteligencia—El Nexo de la Cultura y la Inteligencia Estratégica* (NDIC Press, January 2009) presents that book's introductory material in translation, along with essays by three U.S. and Canadian authors. Essays by the editors and by a Peruvian observer, which make up the introductory material, provide the reader unfamiliar with Spanish or Portuguese an overview of all essays in the original edition. The original book features essays by 28 authors who represent 14 countries in the Western Hemisphere plus Spain. The book aims to educate officials as well as students about the vicissitudes that accompany the development and execution of the government intelligence function. The authors demonstrate that national, strategic intelligence in any country of the Hemisphere can experience episodes of devolution as well as positive evolution, at the same time that the culturally modulated practices of government professionals can oscillate between periods of repression and democratic observance.

Essays by authors who are U.S. Government employees were reviewed and cleared for public release by the Department of Defense's Office of Security Review. This edition and the original book in Spanish and Portuguese are available at *http://www.ndic.edu/press/press.htm*.

Russell G. Swenson, PhD, Director, NDIC Press

CONTENTS

FOREWORD

*Marco Cepik**

This new book edited by Russell Swenson and Susana Lemozy continues and deepens a research partnership that has been useful to the field of intelligence studies in the Americas and beyond. In the wake of contributions such as *Bringing Intelligence About* (Swenson 2003) and *Intelligence Professionalism in the Americas* (Swenson and Lemozy 2004), the editors bring together in this volume 23 essays that address the theme of national culture and its influence on the nature of the intelligence function in 15 countries of the Americas and of Spain.

As the various authors discuss why and how national cultures influence threat perceptions, security and defense policies, and the design of intelligence institutions in their respective countries, readers are treated to more than a description of the intelligence landscape. The editors seize on that auspicious circumstance to formulate a theory about the democratization of the national intelligence function. The theory proposes that the strategic intelligence culture in each country contributes in its own way to the process of democratization, which, in turn, influences the nature of intelligence activities in those countries. This hypothesis is explicit and verifiable. Although it requires additional testing in other national contexts (especially in Africa and Asia), the diverse essays presented here successfully demonstrate the applicability of the concept to Latin America, the United States and Canada, and to Spain.

Research on culture, informal institutions, norms and values associated with intelligence is advanced by this important work, which further develops a line of inquiry that has deep roots in intelligence studies (Jervis, 1985; Lowenthal, 1992; Bozeman, 1992; Boardman, 2006).

Given that intelligence culture depends, for its behavioral expression, on operationalization or codification through individual initiative and collective action, the work presented in this book complements, and does not contradict, institutionally oriented studies that focus on the intelligence function, whether in the military arena or in criminal or police arenas.

|v

---

* Professor of Comparative Politics and International Security at the Federal University of Rio Grande do Sul, Brazil. He holds a doctorate in Political Science and is the author of *Espionagem e Democracia* (Rio de Janeiro, FGV, 2003), as well as four other books and approximately 30 book chapters or journal articles presented in Portuguese, Spanish or English. He also holds a Fellowship with Brazil's National Scientific Research Council.

Several volumes of intelligence case studies have appeared in recent years, many of them centered around well-defined research problems and supported by systematic, empirical evidence (e.g., Herman, 2001, 66-158; Johnson, 2006; Bruneau & Boraz, 2007; Gill & Farson & Phythian & Shpiro, 2008). These works, together with the present volume, are a fuller realization of comparative studies, building on works by the preceding generation of intelligence scholars (e.g., Richelson, 1988; Godson, 1988; Johnson, 1996, 119-145; Herman, 1996, 16-136).

As may be inferred from most of the essays in this book (including the cases of Costa Rica and Colombia as two extremes in terms of the militarization of their intelligence services), the emphasis on State security and control of violent criminal activity is a strong and distinctive feature of the intelligence services across the region. An interesting possibility would be to extend the research carried out for this book to a systematic comparison of the institutional framework and operational emphases in other regions where, as we know through an emerging body of comparative research, there is an impetus to institutionalize democratic reform and improve the integration of law enforcement and strategic intelligence (e.g., Williams & Deletant, 2001; Gill & Brodeur & Tollborg 2003; Born & Johnson & Leigh, 2005; Wetzling, 2006; Gill, 2006; Cepik, 2006; Burch, 2007).

Intelligence studies are on the brink of making the leap to a level where they will have practical relevance. This book edited by Russell Swenson and Susana Lemozy holds importance for its presentation of usefully detailed essays and for the impetus it gives for theoretically oriented comparative studies. The book should be required reading for scholars interested in the combination of intelligence, strategic culture, security and democracy.

References

BOARDMAN, Chase. (2006). "Organizational Culture Challenges to Interagency and Intelligence Community Communication and Interaction." A paper submitted to the Faculty of the Joint Advanced Warfighting School in partial satisfaction of the requirements of a Master of Science Degree in Joint Campaign Planning and Strategy.

BORN, Hans & JOHNSON, Loch & LEIGH, Ian [editors]. (2005). *Who's Watching the Spies: Establishing Intelligence Service Accountability.* Dulles, Virginia, Potomac Books.

BOZEMAN, Adda. (1992). "Knowledge and Method in Comparative Intelligence Studies of the Non-Western World," in BOZEMAN, Adda. *Strategic Intelligence and Statecraft: Selected Essays.* New York, Brassey's, pp. 180-212.

BRUNEAU, Thomas & BORAZ, Steven [editors]. (2007). *Reforming Intelligence: Obstacles to Democratic Control and Effectiveness.* Austin, University of Texas Press.

BRUNEAU, Thomas & DOMBROSKI, Kenneth. (2006). "Reforming Intelligence: the Challenge of Control in New Democracies," in BRUNEAU, Thomas & TOLLEFSON, Scott [editors]. *Who Guards the Guardians and How? Democratic Civil-Military Relations.* Austin, University of Texas Press, pp. 145-177.

BURCH, James. (2007). "A Domestic Intelligence Agency for the United States? A Comparative Analysis of Domestic Intelligence Agencies and Their Implications for Homeland Security," *Homeland Security Affairs*, III, no. 02 (June), pp. 01-26.

CEPIK, Marco & BRUNEAU, Thomas. (2008). "Brazilian National Approach Towards Intelligence: Concept, Institutions and Contemporary Challenges," in GILL, Peter & FARSON, Stuart & PHYTHIAN, Mark & SHPIRO Shlomo [editors]. *Handbook of Global Security and Intelligence: National Approaches.* Vol. 1—The Americas and Asia. Washington, Praeger.

CEPIK, Marco. (2007). "Political Regime and Intelligence System in Brazil: Structural Change and Democratic Control," in BRUNEAU, Thomas C. and BORAZ, Steven [editors]. *Reforming Intelligence: Obstacles to Democratic Control and Effectiveness.* Austin, University of Texas Press, pp. 149-169.

FARSON, Stuart. (1989). "Schools of Thought: National Perceptions of Intelligence," *Conflict Quarterly*, 9, no. 02 (Spring), pp. 52-104.

FRY, Michael G. & HOCHSTEIN, Miles. (1993). "Epistemic Communities: Intelligence Studies and International Relations," *Intelligence and National Security*, 8, no. 3, (July), pp. 14-28.

GILL, Peter & BRODEUR, Jean-Paul & TOLLBORG, Dennis [editors]. (2003). *Democracy, Law, and Security: Internal Security Services in Contemporary Europe.* Aldershot, UK, Ashgate.

GILL, Peter & FARSON, Stuart & PHYTHIAN, Mark & SHPIRO Shlomo [editors]. (2008). *Handbook of Global Security and Intelligence: National Approaches.* Washington, Praeger. ISBN: 0-275-99206-3. [Two vols.]

GILL, Peter. (1994). *Policing Politics: Security Intelligence and the Liberal Democratic State.* London, Frank Cass.

GILL, Peter. (2000). *Rounding Up the Usual Suspects?* Aldershot, UK, Ashgate.

GILL, Peter. (2006). "The Comparative Analysis of Security Intelligence." In JOHNSON, Loch [editor]. *Handbook of Intelligence Studies.* London, Routledge, pp. 82-90.

GODSON, Roy. (1988). Comparing Foreign Intelligence: The U.S., the U.S.S.R., the UK and the Third World. Washington, Brassey's.

HASTEDT, Glenn. (1991). "Towards a Comparative Study of Intelligence," *Conflict Quarterly*, 11, no. 03 (Summer), pp. 55-72.

HENDERSON, Robert. (1995). "South African Intelligence under de Klerk," *International Journal of Intelligence and Counterintelligence*, 8, no. 01 (Spring), pp. 36-56.

HENDERSON, Robert. (2004). *International Intelligence Yearbook,* 2nd edition. Washington, Brassey's.

HERMAN, Michael. (1996). *Intelligence Power in Peace and War.* Cambridge, UK, Cambridge University Press.

HERMAN, Michael. (2001). *Intelligence Services in the Information Age.* London, Frank Cass.

JERVIS, Robert. (1985). "Improving the Intelligence Process: Informal Norms and Incentives." In MAURER, A.C., TUNSTALL, Marion D. & KEAGLE, James M. [editors]. *Intelligence: Policy and Process.* Boulder and London, Westview Press, pp. 113-124.

JOHNSON, Loch [editor]. (2006). *Handbook of Intelligence Studies.* London, Routledge.

JOHNSON, Loch. (1996). *Secret Agencies: U.S. Intelligence in a Hostile World.* New Haven: Yale University Press.

JOHNSON, Loch [editor]. (2006). *Strategic Intelligence.* Washington, Praeger. [Five vols.]

LOWENTHAL, Mark. (1992). "Tribal Tongues: Intelligence Consumers, Intelligence Producers," *Washington Quarterly* (Winter), pp. 157-168.

O'CONNELL, Kevin. (2004). "Thinking about Intelligence Comparatively," *Brown Journal of World Affairs*, vol. II, no. 01 (Summer-Fall), pp. 189-199.

RICHELSON, Jeffrey. (1988). *Foreign Intelligence Organizations.* Cambridge, Massachusetts, Ballinger Publishing Company.

RICHELSON, Jeffrey. (2008). *The U.S. Intelligence Community*, 4th edition. Boulder, Westview Press.

SWENSON, Russell & LEMOZY, Susana. [editors]. (2004). *Intelligence Professionalism in the Americas*, 2nd edition. Washington, Joint Military Intelligence College (JMIC).

SWENSON, Russell [editor]. (2003). *Bringing Intelligence About: Practitioners Reflect on Best Practices.* Washington, JMIC.

TREVERTON, Gregory & JONES, Seth & BORAZ, Steven & LIPSCY, Phillip. (2006). *Toward a Theory of Intelligence: Workshop Report.* Santa Monica, California, Rand Corporation.

WETZLING, Thorsten. (2006). *The Democratic Control of Intergovernmental Intelligence Cooperation.* Geneva, Centre for the Democratic Control of Armed Forces (DCAF), no. 165.

WILLIAMS, Kieram & DELETANT, Dennis. (2001). *Security Intelligence Services in New Democracies: The Czech Republic, Slovakia and Romania.* London, St. Martin's Press.

FRAMEWORK FOR A NORMATIVE THEORY OF NATIONAL INTELLIGENCE

Russell G. Swenson
and
Susana C. Lemozy

The Project

A spy novelist whose words are highlighted by *The Economist* expresses the central theme of this book:

> As that shrewd spy-chronicler, John le Carré, noted once, secret services can be most revealing of the deeper character of the countries they protect. A distinguished British practitioner of the craft recently agreed with him, declaring that intelligence work "is the last expression of national identity and sovereignty."[1]

The present work examines the validity of these observations. In addition, the book aims to determine whether national character can be associated with the nature of national or strategic intelligence in a region of the world much of which lies outside the English-speaking realm. This question remains open and important, given that the intelligence services of any country by definition ideally provide an institutional guarantee of national survival and that strategic intelligence is an indispensable means toward achieving détente or international co-existence. In the end, public consciousness can contribute directly to the positive evolution of this primordial function, which counts as one of the oldest of political institutions, in such a way that we can identify a phenomenon of "democratization" of national intelligence.

The set of essays presented here manifests increasing interest in national-level, government intelligence. Public interest, combined with system-

| 1

---

1 "Cats' Eyes in the Dark," *Economist*, 19 March 2005, p. 32. Unfortunately, the magazine did not reveal the identity of the "distinguished British practitioner," thereby requiring the reader to trust the messenger, ironically like a government report without explicit source documentation. Alberto Bolivar, in an essay in the present volume, also refers to the observation by Le Carré, as presented in *Tinker, Tailor, Soldier, Spy* (New York: Alfred A. Knopf, 1974), p. 342.

atic self-reflection on the national intelligence enterprise by the authors, many of whom are practicing professionals, allow us to operationalize the concept of intelligence democratization. By democratization, we mean the evolutionary process of establishing the rule of law in any given country, whereby specific societal roles are developed for executive, legislative and judicial branches of government, along with the press or mass communications media. We suggest that the democratization of national intelligence comprises the evolution, in any country, of a national system that ranges from the use of an institutional framework to address primarily internal security issues that threaten the survival of *principal* officials of the state (a Security State), to its use to ensure the survival of democratic *principles* in a State of Law as it contends with other countries of the world.[2] We do not intend to judge the value of a system's operating at any given point along this spectrum, but rather to signal the existence of a tendency toward the democratization of this important government function.

The authors of these essays responded to a broad question: How is national culture in your country related to the status and evolution of strategic, national intelligence; and how is the latter practiced, compared to how it should or could be employed? Each author was allowed to apply his or her own interpretation of the concept of "culture." To the editors, the concepts of national culture and national intelligence together constitute a framework of inherited traits and key governmental, institutional adaptations that operate in the context of continual evolution in any society as viewed by its citizenry. The editors requested that the authors focus their efforts on: 1) the concept and application of "culture" within and among the intelligence institutions in the country under examination, and 2) examples of the use of the culture concept to understand and come to grips with national, strategic security problems in the author's own country. As it turned out, the authors went well beyond this initial expectation, which in the end permitted the creation of what we may call a descriptive and normative theory of the "democratization of national intelligence."

---

2 Stuart Farson, in a review article, "Schools of Thought: National Perceptions of Intelligence", *Conflict Quarterly* 9, no. 2 (Spring 1989), pp. 64-66, notes that national police are often identified with intelligence and repression in extreme cases of the first type, whereas on the other extreme, intelligence personnel are often seen as national heroes as they defend democratic principles on the world stage. Available at: *http://www.lib.unb.ca/Texts/JCS/CQ/vol009_2spring1989/Farson.pdf.*

In practice, none of the authors found the concept of a "national intelligence culture" too difficult or too broad to address.[3] As the authors from the various countries responded to requests from the editors to clarify or amplify their points, it became clear that there were several recurring elements in the essays. The degree to which the essays resonated with and resembled each other in several ways was not expected because they were written independently by the authors, with no coordination—authors did not collaborate and for the most part did not know each other until after all essays were accepted and finalized.[4] Following this initial observation, the editors began to search systematically for theoretically significant relationships among these parallel concepts. The framework for a normative theory of intelligence democratization emerged, then, from the editors' review of the collection of essays. Through this theoretical approach, we intend to go beyond a simply descriptive comparison of these essays toward an explanation of similarities and differences in intelligence national culture. In the Table of Contents of the book, we present an outline of this theory through the four-part division of the collective material.

The essays presented here take into account the administrative details that distinguish one state from another among those that share the physical space of the hemisphere, and that also separate the loyalties of citizens. But because only three or four major languages are spoken across the hemisphere,

---

3 The idea of a "national strategic culture" has been addressed regularly since the 1970s by, among others, Colin S. Gray, "Comparative Strategic Culture", *Parameters* (Winter 1984), pp. 26-33; Jeffrey S. Mantis, "Strategic Culture and National Security Policy," *International Studies Review*, vol. 4, no. 3 (Fall 2002), pp. 87-113; and Elizabeth L. Stone and others, *Comparative Strategic Culture: Conference Report*, U.S. Naval Postgraduate School, 21-22 September 2005. However, theoretical development of the concept remains elusive because of the lack of a common definition of key terms and the difficulty of operationalizing relevant variables and their relationship to each other. The present study of national cultures of intelligence attempts to overcome these shortcomings to the degree possible through the presentation of the authentic voices of those with concrete experience in intelligence. The validity of these authors' observations is reinforced by the fact that all of them found it possible to accept joining the concept of culture with that of intelligence.

4 The concept of national cultures of intelligence is being developed in academic journals associated with leading intelligence studies centers. As examples we note: María Teresa Fernández de la Vega, in her Foreword to *Inteligencia y seguridad: Revista de análisis y prospectiva* 1, no. 1 (December 2006), p. 10, writes about "a new culture of intelligence" in Spain; Rafael Martínez develops the concept in "Cultura política sobre inteligencia: Hacia un encuentro con la sociedad," in *Terrorismo global: Gestión de información y servicios de inteligencia*, coords. Diego Navarro Bonilla y Miguel Ángel Esteban (Madrid: Plaza y Valdés, 2007, pp. 165-205; Douglas Porch, in "French Intelligence Culture: A Historical and Political Perspective," *Intelligence and National Security* 10, no. 3 (July 1995), pp. 486-511, and Peter Jackson, in a review essay, "Intelligence and the State: An Emerging 'French School' of Intelligence Studies," *Intelligence and National Security* 21, no. 6 (December 2006), pp. 1061-1065, signal the emergence of academic attention to the distinctive and specifically cultural role of intelligence in French national politics. In the U.S., Michael Turner, in "A Distinctive U.S. Intelligence Identity," *International Journal of Intelligence and Counterintelligence* 17, no. 1 (2004), pp. 42-61, also promotes the concept.

because intelligence specialists share a professional language, and finally because of a widely shared European heritage, it is not surprising that the expression of a governmental function as basic as that of intelligence should be easily recognizable across the entire region. In addition, the European sensibility, we think, is of such a nature that remaining differences will continue to be smoothed over. Therefore, we have some confidence in the validity of the theoretical construction and its applicability across all the countries of the hemisphere.

Schelling[5] confirms that when a social group enjoys a certain level of cohesion among individuals, augmented through the use of a common language, it begins to exhibit predictable behaviors, and we may then reasonably speculate about the group in political and strategic terms, estimating its means, ends and its sense of rationality.[6] We may further judge that a group's attitude toward the future—the arena of national intelligence—is deeply associated with its collective ethos, as suggested by Le Carré. This observation leads us to consider, in view of our authors' work, and for theoretical purposes: To what degree, at the national and strategic level, are underlying socio-cultural issues reflected in the strategic intelligence organizations and practices of particular countries, and further, how are these issues reflected in a country's vision of the future as played out through actions undertaken in the international context? A tentative answer to these questions appears in the divisions applied to the Table of Contents of this book, where we find that respective countries host a range of intelligence systems that first reflect military roots, then evolve through successive organizations to accommodate the interests of civil society that in the end both reflect and create a national culture.

Taking into account the foregoing, the editors now present 22 essays on national culture and national intelligence. Essays focus on 14 long-independent countries of the hemisphere, and are accompanied by an essay from scholars in Spain, the first European colonizing country, which remains a kind of North Star for many people of the Western Hemisphere.

Strategic Intelligence and National Culture

To start down the theoretical path, we can identify the paradigmatic, applied definitions of intelligence and of strategic intelligence shared by government employees throughout the region. Without doubt, during the second

---

5 Thomas C. Schelling, *Micromotivos y macroconducta* (México, Fondo de Cultura Económica, 1989).

6 Susana Lemozy and Daniel Martín Lucatti, "Proyecto Fénix, Problemas de investigación de futuro," IV Parte, *Cuadernos académicos de la Escuela de Defensa Nacional*, Buenos Aires, 2000.

half of the 20th century, the visions of Sherman Kent and Washington Platt[7] were adapted and employed by many in the hemisphere. At the same time, some countries adopted the Soviet intelligence template, itself of European origin. Because of these shared forms, we can expect that the strategic intelligence phenomenon and how it is practiced create a context that allows a comparative assessment of the intelligence systems in all countries of the hemisphere. The possibility of a fuller, including theoretical, development of the concept of strategic intelligence is highlighted by two observers who have thus far been overlooked by students of intelligence.[8] As a result of its theoretical underdevelopment and therefore a lack of effective application, the intelligence services of the United States, at least, are often not successful at combining political knowledge with value-added, processed information that we know as intelligence.[9]

Logically, strategic intelligence can only find a place and opportunity for development among those peoples who have well-defined national interests and a broad societal consensus—a national culture—so that they can expect

7   In his well-known *Strategic Intelligence for American World Policy* (Princeton, NJ: Princeton University Press, 1949), and in Spanish, *Inteligencia estratégica para la política mundial Americana* (Buenos Aires: Círculo Militar, 1951), Sherman Kent offers the paradigm of a body of academic, strategic intelligence specialists, divorced from the political world and focused not on issues internal to their country, but instead exclusively oriented toward foreign targets. Washington Platt, as well, in his *Strategic Intelligence Production* (New York: Frederick A. Praeger, 1957), and in Spanish *Producción de inteligencia estratégica* (Buenos Aires: Editorial Struhart y Cia., 1983), presents his model of military intelligence at the strategic level. Both authors expound a vision of strategic intelligence that excludes or suppresses the contribution of diplomats to the formal process of strategic intelligence. We may deduce from this, and from the evidence presented in the essays in this book, that the definition of strategic intelligence, and the corps of personnel who carry out its process in most countries of the region, arise from these paradigms.

8   One of these is Gregory D. Foster, who in "A Conceptual Foundation for a Theory of Strategy," *The Washington Quarterly* (Winter 1990), pp. 43-48, recognizes that a concept of strategy does not exist separately from a theory of the future (a desired future). This perspective marks as equivalent the concepts of national strategy and strategic intelligence, the latter of which does not make sense unless it is oriented toward a desired, malleable future, necessarily a product of the society's values. The other is Willmoore Kendall, in "The Function of Intelligence," *World Politics* 1, no. 4 (July 1949), pp. 542-552. In this work, which is nothing less than a critical review of Kent's book, Kendall offered a different paradigm—a paradigm that was not adopted by the intelligence services of the United States. He recommended that intelligence analysts and advisors take into explicit account the internal (political) context of the U.S. as a means of understanding strategic challenges and communicating them directly to the highest decision-makers (elected officials) at the national level (pp. 548-550). He also noted (p. 551) the lack of deep and theoretical thinking by Kent, and critically, that the adjective "strategic" when used in association with "intelligence" excludes the larger and more apt concept of "intelligence for foreign policy" (p. 548). The United States, and its intelligence services, in particular on the civilian side, have followed the Kent paradigm, and therefore have not come to address the problem of internal, strategic challenges either in isolation or in relation to external challenges.

9   See Russell G. Swenson, "Visión Política de la Inteligencia Estratégica para los Servicios Nacionales de Las Américas," *Aquimindia* (magazine of the Colombian Administrative Department of Security—DAS) No. 3 (2008), 27-33.

intelligence institutions to remain in place even as the democratic process accords power to political rivals with their own approach to governance. Further, strategic intelligence will flourish only where long-term thinking prevails, and the existence of intelligence organizations is legitimized as an anticipatory response to the need for such thinking.

A clear example of this claim can be seen in the Cuban experience. As articulated by a well-placed and well-informed Cuban commentator, now a resident of the U.S., but for many years an official with that island's intelligence services, "Fidelismo" offers the personification of a "national project" that justifies the existence of the intelligence services, particularly of the Ministry of the Interior (MININT).[10] This intelligence organization, a creation of Fidel Castro and the most respected institution on the island, experiences strong oversight, applied down to the level of individual analysts, by the national leader himself.[11]

The Cuban intelligence system exhibits some other traits distinct from those of other "Western," national services in the hemisphere. According to Menier, Cuban agents, with the conscience and manner of a priest, bring enthusiasm to their field contacts, whereas field operatives in other systems, such as that of the U.S., consider their role necessary, but somewhat distasteful.[12] He also asserts that MININT professionals accomplish their duties with great efficiency, in contrast to those in other, less successful services. What is notable about this comparative glimpse into the Cuban intelligence system is that it allows outsiders to better understand the value as well as the deficiencies of an intelligence bureaucracy, as presented in this book.

Illustrative examples of variables associated with the variety of national intelligence institutions, as developed by the authors, and which create the theoretical context for the democratization of national intelligence

1. *Evolution of the phenomenon of national intelligence*: Breadth of institutional space for the reform of the intelligence enterprise and redirection of its mission; existence, coverage and influence of public literature on intelligence in the social sciences; indepth coverage of intelligence by the press; substantive, public

---

10 Juan Antonio Rodríguez Menier, *Cuba por Dentro* [Inside Cuba] (Miami: Ediciones Universal, 1994).

11 Ibid., pp. 31-33. For a contrasting view of the United States, for example, see Jacob Heilbrunn, "A Lack of Intelligence," *New York Times Sunday Book Review*, 13 April 2008.

12 Ibid., p. 149.

conferences or fora on the theme; laws or directives by the legislative or executive branch; internal or external orientation, or both; degree of tolerance of a loss of privacy because of intelligence activity; i.e., loss of some liberty.

2. *Existence of an intelligence culture*: How the intelligence enterprise is seen within the government and by the larger society—at least by those who are politically aware; strength of attempts to communicate the value of intelligence, by the intelligence services and by their public spokespersons. Degree of freedom of action, with or without official oversight; whether analytic and operational branches of intelligence are combined or kept separate; propensity to sustain (institutionalize) the main mission of intelligence as part of national, strategic planning; education of civilians on the military intelligence culture to facilitate communication between government intelligence personnel and the leading intelligence consumers and political decision-makers; whether an identifiable culture exists among intelligence personnel, even if not at a national level.

3. *Approach to the phenomenon of globalization*: Government intelligence institutions adopt a proactive stance, with an emphasis on innovative application of capabilities to a broad segment of society; or government intelligence functions in a more traditional manner, with an emphasis on identifying targets and addressing them operationally; degree of openness to international intelligence liaison; freedom of intelligence leadership or of field operators to form and maintain international, counterpart relationships. Degree of positive interaction between national intelligence services and police at various levels; also between intelligence and diplomatic officials; tendency to use covert action to promote the development of democratic institutions in societies of the region.

Hypothetical Relationships among Cultural Factors, on the Way to a Theory of Intelligence Democratization

The assertions presented here in three categories take into account the interrelationships of the variables just identified, and are the fabric for a theory of national intelligence in a globalized world.

1. *Origins and evolution of national intelligence*: Certain continuities exist in national intelligence institutions. These continuities correspond to three evolutionary categories or streams.

First and not surprisingly, national intelligence institutions tend to be based on military intelligence precedents; that is, they are strongly hierarchical and assign priority to military-style challenges. What does surprise is that in some cases the national intelligence system leaves the military model behind. From the studies included in this book, we can see that Guatemala, Uruguay and Ecuador are among those countries that have been slow to distance themselves from this model. Among those that can be seen as having put some distance between national intelligence institutions and the military model for intelligence are Chile, Mexico, Argentina and perhaps Colombia. As the Peruvian reviewer observes, in commenting on the work of the Argentinian Sillone, accountability for successes and failures of intelligence can be attributed to civilians as well as the military, and therefore we may consider that the execution of the intelligence function is fully a reflection at large of the country's security establishment. Argentina since 2001 has had in play a legislative act that requires the preparation of civilian professionals in strategic intelligence, in the National Intelligence School.

In the case of Guatemala, as indicated by Capo and Ovalle, a new law in 2008 establishing the framework for a national security system also requires the institutionalization of professional development among civilian intelligence personnel (Ch. 4, Art. 17). This abrupt change away from a military-oriented intelligence model shows that a country can move quickly from one evolutionary category to another. Nonetheless, in countries where the military model remains persistent, we cannot say that national intelligence institutions themselves are strong.

In contrast, we can distinguish a second evolutionary path for national intelligence systems, where intelligence institutions are very strong; that is, publicly accepted and enduring, notwithstanding indications that their operations may not be so effective. These operate in countries that have engaged in wars on the international scene or in internal conflicts lasting more than 10 years: Brazil, Colombia and the United States. Intelligence systems can endure because of the effort required, for example, to exercise control over an extensive national territory. In parallel fashion, they may endure because of a prolonged military-dominated government, as these normally pay close attention to future threats. In Colombia, we see the development of a civil institution, the Administrative Department of Security (DAS) which, as in Brazil, displays an institutionalizing tendency.[13] In the Brazilian case, according to the author Moraes, military influence persists in the realm of national intelligence, being reinforced by the

---

13 Steven C. Boraz, "Intelligence Reform in Colombia: Transparency and Effectiveness against Internal Threats," *Strategic Insights* 6, no. 3 (May 2007). *http://www.ccc.nps.navy.mil/si/2007/May/borazMay07.asp.*

national, civilian intelligence agency (Agência Brasileira de Inteligência) and the intelligence capabilities of the national police, which equal or surpass the resources and capabilities of the military.[14] In the United States, the intelligence system oriented toward internal targets is flourishing, especially in the hands of the new Department of Homeland Security, where, as anticipated by Wiant in another essay, a culture of threat anticipation reigns, as officially acknowledged by the White House.[15] Carrying out an internally focused intelligence mission depends on the efficiency of the new centers at the state level in the U.S. that are to fuse preventive information, as well as on the persistence of information collection by national agencies, especially those that specialize in the interception of communications.[16]

A third category includes those countries traditionally not bellicose, and without military governments, such as Canada and Costa Rica. As affirmed by Lefebvre in the Canadian case, and reinforced by Chaves, who writes about his Central American country, intelligence institutions in these places tend not to have a cultural predilection toward strategic assessment because they lack a formative military legacy. Nevertheless, both authors suggest that there does exist a "circumscribed" intelligence culture among practicing professionals. Mexico may also be placed in this category, according to the analysis by Balcazar. Depending on the strength of each country's respective change agents, intelligence systems may pass from any one of these categories into the next theoretical division, where greater public involvement, or a democratization, of intelligence institutions can generate a national intelligence culture.

2. *Change agents leading to a national intelligence culture:* Several authors address the bureaucratic structure of intelligence in their country and the public oversight required for accomplishing what is beginning to gain some recognition—effective democratization of intelligence. From the senior leaders of intelligence organizations, especially because of a high turnover rate, we see little evidence of the development of a corporate culture, as noted by Torrijos, Serrano y Gomez de la Torre Rotta. The development of an intelligence culture would depend rather on an expansion of the otherwise circumscribed culture

---

14 Marco Cepik y Priscila Antunes, "Brazil's New Intelligence System: An Institutional Assessment," *International Journal of Intelligence and Counterintelligence* 16, no. 3 (Fall 2003), 365-367.

15 President George Bush, The White House, *National Strategy for Homeland Security*, November 2007. *http://www.whitehouse.gov/infocus/homeland/nshs/2007/index.html*, Section VIII, "Culture of Preparedness." Accessed 10 February 2008.

16 Department of Homeland Security, "State and Local Fusion Centers," *http://www.dhs.gov/xinfoshare/programs/gc_1156877184684.shtm* and James Risen and Eric Lichtblau, "Bush Lets U.S. Spy on Callers without Courts," *New York Times*, 16 December 2005. *http://www.nytimes.com/2005/12/16/politics/16program.html*.

nurtured within the intelligence services. Among the change agents that might abet this expansion, we can include commercial books and professional journals that are written and produced by intelligence professionals themselves, even as the publication process, and even if the author is retired from government service, is subject to security oversight.[17]

A similar, literature-based change agent, likewise supporting the democratization of intelligence, arises from autobiographical material related to intelligence. This literature also forges a connection between the intelligence services and the general public, although somewhat less authentically than the direct sources noted above.[18] This literature, often innovative and commercially successful, carries some social value as a means of mass communication on the theme of national intelligence. At a further, academic, remove, we find a series of books that contribute to the objective of public knowledge of the government intelligence world.[19] Finally, intelligence analysts and operatives are also entering the realm of popular culture. In 2007, a famous Brazilian actor and lead character in a *telenovela* played the role of an ABIN agent in the fight against narco-trafficking.[20] These developments are underway after many years of a

---

[17] Among them, for Colombia, see autobiographies by Evelio Buitrago Salazar, *Zarpazo, otra cara de la violencia: Memorias de un suboficial del ejército de Colombia* (Bogotá, 1965), also published as *Zarpazo The Bandit: Memoirs of an Undercover Agent of the Colombian Army*, trans. M. Murray Lasley, ed. Russell W. Ramsey (The University of Alabama Press, 1977), and Jesús Emilio García Acosta, *El Ave del Pantano* [The Bird of the Marsh] (Bogotá, Editorial la Serpiente Emplumada, 2007) (fictionalized account of the author's experiences as an agent of DAS). With respect to the United States, *An Opaque War*, by Frederick Harrison (self-published, 2007), addresses the seam between police intelligence and national security intelligence, and illuminates the decisive moments when front-line supervisors have to choose between continuing to withhold information from counterparts on the other side of the divide, or to undertake preventive actions, a choice that usually is an opportunity and responsibility of the intelligence services themselves.

[18] Examples of this type of literature include: Sergio Aguayo Quezada, *La charola: Una historia de los servicios de inteligencia en México* [The Badge: A History of the Intelligence Services of Mexico] (México: Grijalbo, 2001); Jorge Boimvaser, *Los sospechosos de siempre: Historia del espionaje en la Argentina* [The Usual Suspects: The History of Espionage in Argentina] (Buenos Aires: Planeta, 2001); Lucas Figueiredo, *Ministério do silêncio: a historia do serviço brasileiro de Washington Luis a Lula, 1927-2005* (Rio de Janeiro y São Paulo: Editora Record, 2005). From the United States, and of interest to the hemisphere, see Jefferson Morley, *Our Man in Mexico: Winston Scott and the Hidden History of the CIA* (University Press of Kansas, 2008).

[19] Some that stand out are Diego Navarro Bonilla and Miguel Ángel Esteban Navarro, *Terrorismo global: Gestión de información y servicios de inteligencia* (Madrid: Plaza y Valdés Editores, 2007); Marco Cepik, *Espionagem e democracia* [Intelligence and Democracy] (Rio de Janeiro, Editora FGV, 2003); Priscila Carlos Brandão Antunes, *SNI y ABIN: Uma lectura da actuação dos serviços secretos brasileiros ao longo de século XX* (Rio de Janeiro: Editora FGV, 2002).

[20] According to an anonymous source in ABIN, upon initiating his role in the movie *Segurança nacional* [National Security] (2007), the actor Thiago Lacerda visited the agency and spoke with agents to learn about the context in which agents work, the better to understand how to interpret the role.

prevailing negative image of intelligence operatives, as exemplified by the origin and continued use of the term "araponagem" in Brazil.[21]

What do these vignettes of an intelligence professional's life, and of the institutions that give continuity to a culture of intelligence, really mean? Even though the popular image of intelligence institutions and its operatives may have been negative, for reasons detailed by Figueiredo[22] in the case of Brazil— where intelligence organizations considered certain citizens official enemies largely to protect governing officials from popular retribution—the scene has now shifted noticeably. A major reason is that intelligence institutions now depend on a steady inflow of agents and analysts. The principal message of professionally revealing literature like that mentioned here is positive and promising, and the progenitor of more open studies like the present work. Such studies are multiplying in countries that maintain national intelligence schools, especially ones that focus on education of civilians, as in Argentina, Brazil, Canada, Chile, Colombia and now Peru and the United States, and perhaps about to be developed in Guatemala.

Additionally, today military intelligence is subject to another strong change agent in view of the robust participation of many countries of the hemisphere in peacekeeping operations, either under multilateral auspices or under those of the United Nations. This emerging phenomenon promotes a civilian intelligence sensibility, in this case among the military, which can speed the evolution toward democratization of this governmental function. We may expect that within this international environment there are few doubts about the purpose of intelligence, given that it enjoys a clear operational and strategic purpose in this environment external to the great majority of countries.[23]

3. *National cultures sorted by the nature of their interaction with the globalized world*: We can distinguish three types of society in the hemisphere, according to their democratic climate or environment that might facilitate the development of an intelligence culture at the national or strategic level, as a function of the key phenomenon of the era—globalization. For the politically

---

21 The *araponga*, being a bird with a strident voice, was the name of a Brazilian *telenovela* in 1991 that mocked SNI (National Intelligence Service) agents and treated them with disrespect. The title of the program was a comment on SNI and its operatives, as this bird's ridiculously loud voice was the precise opposite of the silence expected of professional intelligence operatives. Earlier, in the United States, a somewhat similar message came with the 1965-70 television show *Get Smart*, as it also made fun of intelligence operatives.

22 Figueiredo, p. 16.

23 See Ben de Jong, Wies Platje and Robert David Steele, eds., *Peacekeeping Intelligence: Emerging Concepts for the Future* (Oakton, Virginia: OSS International Press, 2003), and Eduardo Aldunate Herman, *Misión en Haití: Con la mochila cargada de esperanzas* [Mission in Haiti: With a Knapsack Full of Hope] (Santiago: Centro de Estudios Bicentenario, 2007).

aware population, as well as for other citizens, with respect to government intelligence activities, it is no longer possible to separate the internal from the international environment. Naturally, this is because of the transnational nature of recognizable threats.

As a first type, we can single out those societies primarily oriented toward a self-centered realism and infused with a strong pragmatic streak. Intelligence institutions in such societies exhibit, as a cultural trait, behaviors that place great value on present-day priorities, which in the case of the United States translates to heavy dependence on technical means of intelligence collection, as explained here by Miller.[24] In another society, the government of Costa Rica, according to Chaves, does not possess a strategic intelligence institution of any description. Therefore, by definition, any potential strategic threat would remain unrecognized. For countries such as Costa Rica, which lack a perception of external threats, and lack the institutions that could address such threats, even their pragmatism would not ensure fruitful international exchanges of intelligence, nor even an exchange of actionable information with such agencies as INTERPOL, which would indicate a pragmatic accommodation with globalization.

This mode of thinking and behavior corresponds, at the collective level, with policies that give priority to short-term results. These societies often reveal a certain blindness to the probable global consequences of their actions (for the United States, we have the example of the invasion of Iraq).[25] On occasion, the lack of a future perspective can lead to a repetition of errors, which in turn can create a vicious cycle whereby a discussion of past errors and a search for those historically culpable can further obscure new, global opportunities for the medium and long term. We may also infer that some countries have passed through this stage en route to a more refined intelligence culture. For example, in the Central American region, we now see a contrasting situation between

---

24 The centrality of pragmatism in the culture of the United States is the abiding theme of the book by political scientist John W. Kingdon, *America the Unusual* (Boston: St. Martin's, 1999). See especially chapter 5.

25 Although the U.S. Intelligence Community produces its well-known National Intelligence Estimates, it is also well-known that political leaders can ignore estimates that contradict their own preferences. A concrete example comes from the U.S. Intelligence Community, which did produce two estimates that foresaw in detail the results of the invasion of Iraq. These estimates were clearly politicized, some months before the invasion, as documented in the *Report of the Select Committee on Intelligence on Prewar Intelligence Assessments about Postwar Iraq* (Washington, DC: U.S. Senate, 110th Cong. 1st Sess., 25 May 2007), available (edited version) en *http://www.intelligence.senate.gov/prewar.pdf*. The Executive Branch either rejected or ignored the estimates, as recounted by a participant, Paul Pillar, in "Inside track: Sometimes the CIA is right," *The National Interest Online*, 6 June 2007, at *http://www.nationalinterest.org/Article.aspx?id=14564* and by journalist David Ignatius, "When the CIA Got It Right," *Washington Post*, 23 September 2007, B7. *http://www.washingtonpost.com/wp-dyn/content/article/2007/09/21/AR2007092101941.html*.

Guatemala and Costa Rica. As noted, Guatemala has a new intelligence law that establishes the institutional basis for national decisions through a formal, national intelligence system.[26] Costa Rica still does not.

As a second type of society, we can suggest that those firmly grounded by a socio-economic foundational myth, and that can imagine or sense clear challenges to that foundation, including those associated with the strong winds of globalization, and with values widely shared through the society, typically show a tendency to develop strategic security plans, or strategic planning,[27] even if not precisely "strategic intelligence."[28] As Sancho Hirane notes, in her study of Chile, we need to differentiate strategic planning from strategic intelligence, since planning at the national level deals with actions to be taken to achieve specific objectives, whereas strategic intelligence is oriented toward the process of handling information and its interpretation with the aim of aiding (often emergency) decision making by the highest (elected) officials.

With their promising mixture of pragmatism and patriotic idealism, the intelligence culture of this second group of societies can be associated with globalization in some interesting ways. A strong tendency to observe foundational values at any cost can bring these societies at times to achieve success on the international stage through the effective use of intelligence institutions. For example, as Balcazar observes, the evolution of government intelligence services in Mexico, supported by a recognized intelligence culture, has led to the reinstatement of intelligence professionals, many of whom were earlier and unjustifiably let go from their posts. This positive development leads Serrano to comment that the maturity of experienced intelligence personnel like those back in place in Mexico brings an opportunity for the fruitful development of "more direct channels for the deepening of cooperation among counterpart, foreign agencies as they together confront transnational threats." That is, in well-grounded societies, there is institutional space for the parallel development of globalization of the intelligence function.

---

26 Congreso de la República de Guatemala, Decreto Número 18-2008, published in *Diario de CentroAmérica*, 15 April 2008, no. 12, Vol. 284. *http://www.congreso.gob.gt/gt/leyes2.asp?year=2008*.

27 Periodically, governments of South and Central America publish "White Books" that are strategic planning documents for defense and national security. In the Brazilian case, as noted by Sancho Hirane, the Office of the President published the "Projeto Brasil 3 Tempos 50 Temas Estratégicos" [Project Brazil: 50 Strategies in Three Stages] (Brasil: Presidência da Republica, Núcleo de Assuntos Estratégicos, 2006). Ver en *http://www.resdal.org/ultimos-documentos/main-brasil-estrategia-def-06.html*.

28 In his essay, the Argentine author Auel suggests that as a contributor to strategic planning, strategic intelligence needs to be institutionalized. In his view, this approach would establish and maintain a degree of "cultural empathy" toward the true foundational roots of the country, which may otherwise be lost.

It is also important to recognize that many countries of the hemisphere make a conscious strategic decision when they choose to participate with military forces in multilateral peace operations, under the flag of the United Nations or in rescue missions following natural disasters, under a regional security organization like the Organization of American States. There exists no place in the international scene better than these for a country to burnish its reputation as a participant in the global context. Further, intelligence services should play an important part in these activities, as noted by several of the authors whose work appears in the book Peacekeeping Intelligence,[29] and which addresses the role of intelligence in peace operations. At the strategic/political level, as suggested by an Israeli author, intelligence services that participate in peace operations can become a tool for the conduct of international relations, by virtue of their capacity to conduct negotiations behind the scenes toward the advancement of political possibilities for the maintenance of peace, backed as they are by deployed forces.[30] This point is reinforced by the comment of an Argentine observer who describes how participants in peace operations play a role in diplomacy, even as formally accredited diplomats are now being withdrawn from deployment.[31]

Furthermore, from the perspective of a Chilean Army general who led the peacekeeping force (MINUSTAH) in Haiti, there is a great opportunity in multilateral missions for the development and application of skills by intelligence personnel, especially in the analysis area.[32] In this environment, intelligence personnel can develop their own combination of pragmatic and idealistic capabilities, and given that many of these individuals, from all participating countries, continue on in the intelligence career field, as civilian analysts or operatives in the national intelligence services, the intelligence culture in the respective countries will also grow.

In terms of their intelligence culture, this second type of society occupies an intermediate position between those with a strong streak of pragmatism, on one hand, and those with a more utopian bent.

29 Ben deJong, Wies Platje, y Robert David Steele, *Peacekeeping Intelligence*, pp. 15, 63.

30 Shlomo Shpiro, in *Peacekeeping Intelligence*, p. 112.

31 See Albino Gómez, "Debilidad de la actual diplomacia", Noticias, No. 1622 de *Perfil.com*, 25 enero del 2008. *http://www.revista-noticias.com.ar/comun/nota.php?art=1076&ed=1622*.

32 Eduardo Aldunate Herman, pp. 254-268. Included among countries of the hemisphere with military personnel deployed to Haiti were Argentina, Brazil, Ecuador, Perú, Uruguay and Bolivia.

A third category of countries, in terms of their approach to globalization, gives full play to ideological elements in the development of an intelligence culture, without the moderation afforded by a complement of pragmatism or "democratization." These are the societies where "revanchist" forces seek to regain or justify the reinstatement of their own exclusive priorities, which, in intelligence terms, includes the use of intelligence services to "spy" on the country's own citizens and residents. Several countries in the hemisphere have experienced, as a result of revanchism, periodic, wholesale dismissal of analysts as well as operatives, among them the U.S., Argentina, Brazil, Cuba, Mexico and Peru. These episodes engender a public disrespect for intelligence services which is difficult to overcome, because intelligence services typically do not enjoy a deep reservoir of support, or even strong spokespersons, deficiencies which correspond with a weak national intelligence culture. We may expect that this erroneous, anti-democratic, utopian approach can bring repeated episodes of revanchism, with undoubted costs globally, where the perception of the country is of unending, abrupt changes in policy. Contrary to expectations, Cuba, as a supposed bastion of utopianism, in fact has highly pragmatic national intelligence services, according to a separate study by Menier. On this island, MININT personnel can count on more than token pragmatism in their interaction with the "maximum leader" if there exists conflict between exploiting information advantages and following the path of ideological purity.[33] Thus, we see that a society with a healthy dose of pragmatism can escape the trap of utopian idealism, even in the intelligence arena, in the face of global realities.

The important thing to recognize about these three categories—of a country's approach to globalization, and the associated intelligence culture—is that countries can and do move from one category to another over time, depending on the tendencies of the political regime. Therefore, it remains important to keep a close eye on change agents, as they express and enforce normative and democratic ideas.

---

33 Menier, *Cuba por Dentro*, p. 57.

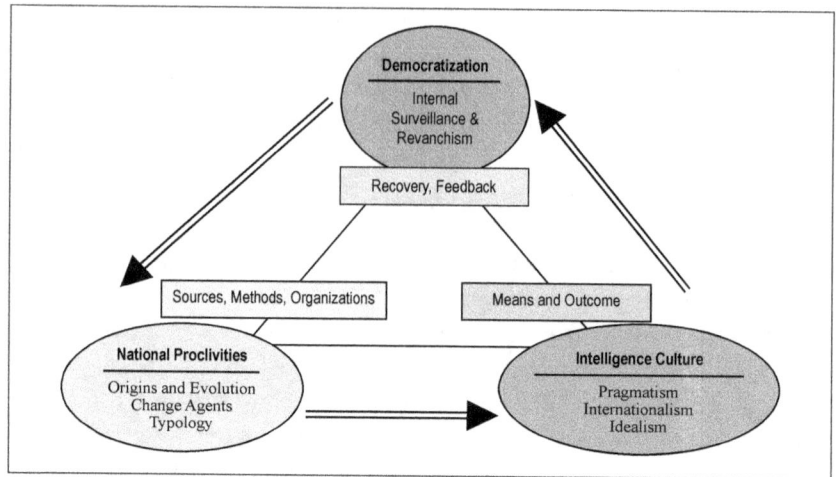

Cyclic Model of National Intelligence Democratization Process.
Source: The editors, modified from concepts presented in Sancho Hirane, in the Spanish/Portuguese volume.

As indicated in the graphic model of this rudimentary, descriptive theory, among the three apexes of the triangle—Proclivities, Culture and Democratization—only the latter is the locus of continuous, influential change, with the ideas of Recovery and Feedback energizing the entire cycle from outside the intelligence enterprise itself. As indicated graphically, the problem of internal surveillance, along with revanchism, represent overlapping foci of democratization. The cyclical nature of the process that mediates between the intelligence enterprise and popular democracy is emphasized by the concepts associated with each apex of the triangle: Intelligence Culture exists as an Outcome of a particular combination of Sources, Methods and Organizations. At the same time, that culture offers the Means for the public to interpret how the national intelligence system operates as it seeks democratic adjustments in the system.

Implications of the Proposed Theory of National Intelligence Democratization

1. The theory can show us how not to impede the positive evolution of national intelligence.

The experience of several countries signals the importance of avoiding the problem of "starting from zero" when a large number of intelligence personnel, analysts or operators are summarily dismissed from employment. Especially when a service is not very large, it is clearly important to keep second-tier employees in the service as a means of ensuring continuity of operations. Through this employment strategy, sources can be maintained and useful methods of analysis, collection and field tradecraft can be preserved. The institution most suited to maintain a high level of professionalization in these circumstances is a national intelligence school, whether civilian or military.[34] Once a school is closed, positive evolution ends.

Looking toward the future, and applying this normative theory, the Spanish example can be emulated. According to the essay by Velasco et. al. in this book, that national intelligence system, complete with democratic, public participation, exemplifies an advanced expression of intelligence culture. At least, we can consider that this European state, mother country and now sister state to many of the Western Hemisphere's polities, with common language ties, offers a positive model for the continuous development of national intelligence systems.

2. The theory helps us understand how intelligence culture relates to perceived threats to national existence.

As anticipated by the theory of democratization of the intelligence function developed here, in a world of existential threats that have spread globally, national intelligence has been transformed from the military model of preparation for defensive wars into a "public" intelligence that requires permanent vigilance, especially given the lack of time available under many circumstances for strategic planning and the need for anticipatory decision making by civilian, public officials.[35] Among the authors who develop this theme in the present work is Sancho Hirane, who writes of intelligence as an inherently democratic, "public service." Under this framework, the purpose of government intelligence services is to ensure the existence of a pluralistic, national, civic infrastructure, rather than of a particular regime or political party currently in power. Reyes-Alonso brings us to understand, at the same time, and in contrast to the inefficiencies of a system oriented to public service, the great efficiency and effectiveness of intelligence systems expressly oriented toward the survival of a highly personalist arrangement such as the "fidelista" regime of Cuba. The phenomenon at play in both cases can be labeled "intelligence for peacetime," given the continuous need to take action against daily challenges.

---

34 Russell G. Swenson, "¿Qué puede ser una Escuela Nacional de la Inteligencia?" (What a National Intelligence School Can Be) *AAinteligencia*, 1, no. 3 (Marzo 2008), pp. 54-59.

35 The principal voice arguing for greater democratization of intelligence in the U.S., Robert Steele, continues to develop the theme of "public intelligence" in *The New Craft of Intelligence: Personal, Public and Political* (Oakton, Virginia: OSS International Press, 2002) and *Collective Intelligence: Creating a Prosperous world at Peace* (Oakton, Virginia: Earth Intelligence Network, 2008).

For the United States, the reorientation of intelligence toward permanent vigilance is rooted in the Cold War of the 20th century, as expressed in this passage:

> It is now clear that we are facing an implacable enemy whose avowed objective is world domination by whatever means and at whatever cost. There are no rules in such a game.... If the United States is to survive, long-standing American concepts of "fair play" must be reconsidered. We must develop effective espionage and counterespionage services and must learn to subvert, sabotage and destroy our enemies by more clever, more sophisticated and more effective methods than those used against us. It may become necessary that the American people be made acquainted with, understand and support this fundamentally repugnant philosophy.[36]

Of course, not all senior officials agreed with this assessment.[37] Nonetheless, this call for public buy-in for more robust intelligence actions signals a decisive change in the U.S. national intelligence culture, especially on the internal or domestic front, a change subsequently reinforced by a renewed focus on intelligence for internal security in reaction to the events of 11 September 2001.

In another part of the Hemisphere, with respect to democratization of national intelligence, we find in Chile an interesting example of a public exchange between alleged internal surveillance by intelligence services and revanchist opponents.[38] The article alleges surveillance of environmental, non-government organizations by the Chilean national intelligence system. If the allegation is accurate, from an optimistic point of view, such surveillance would

---

36 James H. Doolittle, "The Report on the Covert Activities of the Central Intelligence Agency, September 30, 1954," 40, quoted in Richard A. Best, Jr. and Herbert Andrew Boerstling, Appendix C, CRS Report: Proposals for Intelligence Reorganization 1949-1996 (A Report Prepared for the Permanent Select Committee on Intelligence, House of Representatives) and presented in *IC21: The Intelligence Community in the 21st Century*, Permanent Select Committee on Intelligence Staff Study, House of Representatives, One Hundred Fourth Congress, 28 February 1996. *http://www.access.gpo.gov/congress/house/intel/ic21/ic21018.html*.

37 Two members of a covert actions oversight commission put in place by President Eisenhower remained opposed to this change because of continuing absence of strong oversight. See Peter Grose, *Gentleman Spy: The Life of Allen Dulles* (Boston: Houghton Mifflin, 1994), pp. 445-448.

38 "ANI recluta experto para monitorear conflictos y a ONG ambientalistas" (Chilean National Intelligence Employs Expert to Monitor Conflicts and Environmentalist NGOs), *La Tercera* (Santiago), 7 December 2007, p. 26. This allegation, because it was neither admitted nor discussed more thoroughly by accusers, can be characterized as only potentially "revanchist." In the case of Brazil, as noted in the essay by Moraes, today former revanchists receive pensions to repay earlier, inappropriate surveillance of their actions by national intelligence elements.

allow the intelligence services to remain aware of developments within the country, in a more efficient fashion than through the examination of second-hand or "processed" information about the social environment. Of note, when communication channels remain open among the various participants in a case like this, without restrictions, we see democratization of national intelligence in action.

From Brazil, another example highlights the multi-faceted responsibility to address ongoing democratization of national intelligence. In open discussion, an advisor on intelligence affairs to the Brazilian Congress, Joanisval Brito Goncalves (also a contributing author to the present book), counsels: "Considering that the public perception of intelligence is linked to oppressive political regimes...the legitimacy of the Brazilian National Intelligence Service will emerge through actions that promote a *culture of intelligence* not only within government organizations, but also in the private sector, where there is a need to spot threats, such as industrial espionage, and in the end, to have in place a system to address those threats."[39]

The theory allows us to address a presumed rule: that the more regimented societies harbor national intelligence services oriented toward internal targets, whereas the intelligence services of countries that are more politically open tend to focus outside the homeland. As shown by several authors in this book, including those from the U.S., military as well as civilian intelligence operatives at times focus internally. A corollary of the rule would be that the level of democratization of national intelligence would be diminished where internal surveillance is strongest. But do these presumed rules hold up under closer examination?

We can begin with a question: How could we address the concept of intelligence democratization in the context of threat perception? We could contrast the national intelligence systems of two countries in the hemisphere thought to represent opposite extremes: Cuba and the United States. From the civilian perspective, we would right away realize that the two intelligence cultures do not display the simple and clear distinctions we would expect. For example, in the United States, cultural acceptance of an intelligence ethic usually associated with foreign, antagonistic states, after 11 September 2001 was extended to an approval of internal surveillance by national intelligence organizations, notwithstanding the revanchist complaints of principal civil liber-

---

39 Presidencia da Republica, Gabinete de Seguranca Institucional, III Encontro de estudos: *Desafios para a atividadede inteligencia no seculo XXI* (Intelligence Challenges of the 21st Century), Brasilia, 2004, pp. 143-144. Italics in the passage were added by the editors.

ties organizations.[40] Authorization of internal surveillance in the United States is based on the philosophy embodied in the President's Homeland Security Strategy, where the Bush Administration announced its intention to put in place a "culture of preparedness," as noted earlier. Naturally, this philosophy is under continuous debate in the larger society, as expected by the theory set forth here.

On the other hand, in Cuba, and in Venezuela, where the Cuban approach remains a desired option by President Chavez, the democratic ethic consists of widespread, systematic observation and reporting on the behavior of neighbors and family members whose actions or plans may be seen as anti-Presidential.[41] If there exists a real distinction between the two cases, it would be that in Cuba the intelligence focus remains on protecting the nation, which under "fidelismo" is the same thing as the political regime. For the United States, the legitimacy of the internal information net rests on the sense that the state is being protected, but not necessarily the political regime.[42] Despite increased internal surveillance by intelligence services, rather than being diminished in the U.S., a powerful impetus toward increased democratization of intelligence generates an atmosphere that allows repeated leaks of intelligence reporting and subsequent public commentary on the ultimate strategic intelligence documents, the renowned National Intelligence Estimates.

For the most part, the national intelligence services in countries across the hemisphere are oriented primarily toward the internal environment. The continued march of globalization may become a change agent in this arena, with a reorientation toward a greater outward focus corresponding to the degree

---

40 For example, the American Civil Liberties Union (ACLU) published *The Surveillance-Industrial Complex: How the American Government Is Conscripting Businesses and Individuals in the Construction of a Surveillance Society* (2004), available at *http://www.aclu.org/FilesPDFs/surveillance_report.pdf*. The fears expressed by the ACLU are associated with a Federal Bureau of Investigation program called InfraGard, aimed at collaborating on infrastructure protection (*http://www.infragard.net/*) with the National Applications Office of the Department of Homeland Security, which manages the coordination of internal surveillance in the U.S. See *http://www.dhs.gov/xnews/releases/pr_1187188414685.shtm*. At the same time, the issue of private sector surveillance by Internet Service Providers, among others, is also beginning to surface. See Paul Ohm, "The Rise and Fall of Invasive ISP Surveillance," 30 August 2008, available at *http://ssrn.com/abstract=1261344*.

41 Menier, op. cit., p. 51. This author asserts that "The agents in Cuba who produce the bulk of operational intelligence information used by the different branches of the Ministry (MININT) number about 500,000 individuals. The so-called "frozen" sources—those whose services can be accessed when necessary—approach three million (in a country of eleven million residents).

42 Evidence is presented that numerous youths and even famous partisans of leftist organizations in the United States participated knowingly and willingly as government informants in "front organizations" of the CIA for many years during the Cold War, in Hugo Wilford, *The Mighty Wurlitzer: How the CIA Played America* (Cambridge: Harvard University Press, 2008). Their actions were self-justified by patriotic concerns that transcended partisan political alignment.

to which the government of a country recognizes the significance of financial interests from abroad. A lesson emerges here for national intelligence services and their respective governments, whether open or regimented: It is unwise to overlook the primarily internal orientation of counterpart intelligence services, nor to underestimate the importance of this internal orientation as a source of insight into perceived threats. Thus, we see still another rationale for international cooperation among intelligence services: to gain further understanding of the foreign internal environment, and of the degree of sincerity with which that environment is represented by the respective intelligence services among the foreign countries of interest. The predominantly internal orientation allows us to understand with some perspective the observation about national intelligence being a mirror of national culture, as presented in the *Economist* article of 2005 (see footnote 1 above).

To the extent that internally focused intelligence is carried out by police forces rather than intelligence services, and concentrated on the prosecution of past events rather than the prevention of future threats, there will remain an important, internal role for national intelligence of a political/military nature. On that note, Farson suggests that we should engage in close study of cases involving internal surveillance that cross the usual divide between police and national security intelligence. He recommends in particular studying the long-standing, collaborative engagement by British police and national intelligence forces in Northern Ireland.[43]

3. The theory permits a balanced consideration of some profound questions.

Until now, some questions about personal and national security have been considered too difficult to contemplate, let alone resolve, through the formal intelligence infrastructure. For example:

1) Do national leaders and intelligence officials, who bear responsibility for the survival of the society, need an "enemy" or an "other" on which to focus their efforts? Or could a strong and broad culture of intelligence reinforce an alternative orientation toward the recognition and promotion of a society's central values through a more positive concept, such as identifying and reducing obstacles to the universal observation of human rights?

The accomplishment of this vision would not imply the end of clandestine or even covert operations, but that their objective (at a general level) be known and discussed in the public domain as suggested by the model rep-

---

43 Farson, op. cit., p. 80.

resenting the democratization of this government function. The recognition of human rights issues would be of the greatest importance in this discussion to avoid the situation in recent Cuban history, where, according to Menier, MININT personnel focused efficiently on internal enemies whose cases were resolved not by a judicial system, but personally by Fidel.[44] At the same time, much of the world considers indefensible the U.S. detention over a prolonged period without due legal process, on another part of the Cuban island, of the "enemy combatants" at Guantanamo Bay.[45] These detentions are defended as a way of obtaining intelligence data. In the end, it may be that we still are not able to propose a positive response to these questions. At the least, they are questions that demand consideration in a democratic context.

2) To establish an efficient and legitimate intelligence system, do we need transparent accountability of intelligence institutions as well as for key individuals within these institutions?

As related by Menier, accountability to an ultimate decision maker like Fidel confers a robust efficiency to the work of personnel at all levels of the Interior Ministry in Cuba. He adds that in his experience, this accountability required that Fidel be told unvarnished "truths," whether it was good or bad with respect to his policies, with no untoward repercussions on the career of the messenger.[46] In other societies, accountability among intelligence personnel has been generally less direct and less robust, with the effect of allowing more liberty to professionals as they carry out their duties.[47] The evolution of intelligence systems and the concomitant development of democratization, according to the model presented here, will allow intelligence personnel to balance the liberty of individual initiative in taking on strategic topics that are beyond the immediate interests of the society's political leaders, and the benefits of a close, invited relationship with leaders that might not allow for errors or judgment in presenting "the unvarnished truth." Clearly, direct, long-term accountability of intelligence institutions and their key officials is not common, yet without it there is too easy disregard of strategic intelligence systems by elected officials.

[44] Menier, *Cuba por dentro*, pp. 46-48, 57-58. In a well-known instance—the purge of 1989-90 – he witnessed the jailing of the Minister of the Interior José Abrantes, and the firing squad death of General Ochoa. According to Menier, both these individuals recognized the unavoidable necessity of change in Cuban politics, that is, of Fidel's policies.

[45] See Andy Worthington, *The Guantánamo Files: The Stories of the 759 Detainees in America's Illegal Prison* (London: Pluto Press, 2007).

[46] Menier, *Cuba por dentro*, p. 45.

[47] See Hans Born, Loch K. Johnson, and Ian Leigh, *Who's Watching the Spies: Establishing Intelligence Service Accountability* (Washington, DC: Potomac Books, 2005), a normative study of nine countries from around the world. Also see Loch K. Johnson, "The Contemporary Presidency: Presidents, Lawmakers, and Spies: Intelligence Accountability in the United States," *Presidential Studies Quarterly*, 43, no. 4 (December 2004), pp. 828-837.

The concept of a democratization of intelligence systems, bringing transparency and a society's sense of fairness to expectations and repercussions, can encourage a more serious application of accountability.

What Value Does a Theory of Democratization of National Intelligence Deliver?

National organizations and systems of intelligence serve nearly everywhere to monitor, project and often to prevent or counteract sources of threat, whether internal or external. To the extent these organizations and systems operate from the shadows, a theory that tries to shed light on intelligence processes depends heavily on the heretofore unpublished observations of practitioners. As noted in the Lefebvre essay, it can be difficult to create a national intelligence culture when the *form* of addressing the intelligence environment (because of ideological factors rooted in strategic culture) largely overshadows the true *substance* that comes from a consideration of the realities of international power relationships. The model that portrays the present, normative intelligence theory acts as a reminder of the parallelism and needed balance among the three bases of democratization—the three foundations of democratic societies—the executive, legislative and judicial branches. The development of this theory of national intelligence lies precisely on this foundation. The executive role is recognized as a function of democratization itself, the legislative through the self-organization and ethical actions of intelligence professionals and their organizations. A new perspective developed in this book, and highlighted in the descriptive theory, is the development of the concept that a country's national intelligence culture modulates the de facto legal or juridical perception of intelligence through the history of any given society.

Like any social science theory, that presented here offers definitions, a review of variables associated with the intelligence function from a cultural perspective, and a categorization of national intelligence institutions in cultural context. The formulation explains how pertinent variables relate to one another, highlights the evidence of evolutionary development trends in national intelligence, and generates a model to facilitate a projection of how those trends will continue to evolve. As the future unfolds, the theory may remain adequate or may not, depending on the influence of a growing interest in and commitment to national intelligence. At the least, we can expect an evolution of national intelligence services that will offer ideas suitable for scientific research, leading perhaps to a more empirical theory of national intelligence. As suggested by Farson, for example, causal relationships among the contents of intelligence databases, policy formation, and covert action remain to be explored and characterized.[48] Because an empirical theory will be based on existing—that is, historical—data, it may be that the present normative theory, to the degree that it focuses on the present and future, will motivate some individuals to undertake democratic action with respect to their country's intelligence services. The present theory can lead them to understand, categorize and evaluate existing and potential interrelationships among variables, which exist in an action space that is both dependent on detail and always undergoing change.

Point of Departure

It is commonly noted, especially among experienced personnel, that an individual's character reveals itself most clearly when the individual is in a situation of extreme danger, such as on the battlefield, and we may expect the same to be true in the realm of strategic intelligence when the state and its leaders find themselves in critical situations. Referring once again to the initial paragraph of this essay, where independent voices from the humanities present the claim that intelligence services reveal the true nature of the larger society, we can infer that there exists a long-term, institutional or cultural interrelationship between the intelligence services and the states they serve. In the essays presented here the strong tendency of authors, each acting independently, was to ground their work in the national history of their country as they addressed the task at hand. The intelligence function, whether viewed from the perspective of an individual or a nation-state, being by definition the first and last means of ensuring survival through its capacity to combat competing actors and other existential challenges, can be understood through humanistic, literary formulations as well as through the historical lens. We believe that the combination of humanistic and scientific viewpoints, the latter being presented in this book and representing the long experience of nation-states, gives full support to the concept that individual liberty, the nature of the intelligence function, and the participatory democracy enjoyed by many states of the region together promote a positive, evolutionary outlook across the hemisphere.

---

48 Farson, op. cit., p. 80.

About the Authors

Beginning in 1989, **Susana C. Lemozy** worked as professor and academic advisor at the Argentine Army Senior War College, then at the Army Intelligence School. From 2000 to 2006, she taught and served as academic advisor for the Armed Forces Joint Intelligence Institute. She is now in charge of the Applied Intelligence Division of the Institute's Research Department. She is author of several publications on intelligence and future-focused analytic methods for the defense establishment. She holds a degree in political science from the Universidad del Salvador, Buenos Aires, where she has also worked as professor. Email: *lemozy@fibertel.com.ar.*

Russell G. Swenson served from 1988 as professor, and from 1995 as Director of Applied Research at the National Defense Intelligence College. He also directed the NDIC Press. He is author and editor of numerous publications on intelligence process (*http://www/ndic.edu/press/press.shtm*). In earlier years, he worked as intelligence analyst and linguist in the U.S. Air Force and as professor of Geography at Western Illinois University. He holds undergraduate degrees from the University of Kansas (Geography, Spanish, Latin America Area Studies) and from the University of Wisconsin-Milwaukee (Masters and Doctorate in Geography). Following his retirement in 2008, he continues international collaboration with officials and researchers in the field of strategic intelligence. Email: *Rgswenson@gmail.com.*

INVITED COMMENTARY

Jorge Serrano Torres

This book addresses "National Culture and Strategic Intelligence in the Americas," and its view of the historical evolution and current situation of intelligence services of the region is without precedent. The work complements the 2004 book, *Intelligence Professionalism in the Americas*, edited by the same team. All the authors take on the question: How does the national culture of the countries in the Americas relate to the status, evolution, and practice of strategic intelligence there?

If it is possible to accept that there is no authentic liberty without security, nor true security without liberty, then the development of a dynamic and vigorous culture of security and intelligence ought to be inherent to modern societies, which Ulrich Beck has characterized as "societies at risk"[49] because of the new and complex threats which they face in an interdependent and constantly evolving world.

Given that national culture by definition influences the way in which each country confronts strategic problems of security, the present book is a valuable contribution to disentangling the role of culture in the evolution, the deterioration, and the interrelationship of the systems and services of national intelligence, as well as its role in the production of strategic intelligence. It is better still for presenting the diverse views of the distinguished authors whose work is brought together in this text. They accomplish the objective of analyzing the central question of the book in an overall comparative manner, which invites the reader to consider the theme more deeply.

As a result, we are able to see that nearly all the national intelligence services, to a greater or lesser degree, face a critical juncture: They must adjust to more adequately confront the new risks and threats of the 21st century.[50] For this, they need to construct privileged channels of communication in the world of intelligence, in academic and scientific communities, among experts in security and, of course, to secure legitimacy, in the society in general. In this

---

49 Ulrich Beck, *La Sociedad del riesgo: Hacia una nueva modernidad* (Barcelona: Editorial Paidós, 1994).

50 David J. Kilcullen, "New Paradigms in the Conflicts of the 21st Century, *eJournal USA*. Available at *http://usinfo.state.gov/journals/itps/0507/ups/kilcullen.htm*.

context, they need to acquire new ways of working, principally by developing a culture of active coordination within the national scene as well as the international environment.

The concepts covered by the authors generate interest, showing that eclectic, strategic points of view can highlight shared patterns and processes as well as the particular phenomena that characterize the different communities of intelligence of the region. Taking into account the overall picture makes it possible to discern elements of intersection or perhaps symbiosis that emerge between the concepts of "national culture" and "national intelligence." Equally, however, and at the other extreme, it becomes apparent that the absence of a strongly rooted culture of security and intelligence remains a difficult obstacle to the achievement of greater institutionalization, professionalism, and operational efficiency of the national intelligence services, which are indispensable for successfully confronting the problems of national and regional strategic security.

The Peruvian Case: Consequences of an Absent Culture of Security and National Intelligence

> *The legend says that an eagle who was shot through by an arrow considered the feathered dart and said: it is no other than our own plumage that has now impaled us (Aeschylus, excerpts).*

Nothing other than this excerpt could better reflect the destruction which the intelligence system of Peru has suffered, at the hands of the Peruvians themselves, in recent decades. The essays by my Peruvian compatriots, Andrés Gómez de la Torre Rotta and Alberto Bolívar Ocampo, confirm that the Peruvian population has not yet succeeded in understanding that security, defense, and intelligence are public services destined to preserve the existence of the nation. Despite the fact that this understanding has not been fully assimilated, there is in our society a general appreciation for the values of democracy and respect for human rights.

The absence of a rooted culture of security and national intelligence persists, despite the efforts of the National Accord in the year 2002,[51] where, with the participation of many of the institutions of organized society and the State itself, 31 policies were created, the ninth of which was devoted to national security. Further, a national security culture remained unrealized

---

[51] See *Documentos del Acuerdo Nacional.* Available online at *http:/www.acuerdonacional. gob.pe/DocumentosAN/documentos.htm.*

even after March 2004, when the National Defense Council put in place a National Policy for Security and Defense.[52]

Despite these positive developments, there remain in Peru many obstacles to achieving social cohesion, namely: strengthening pride in national identity; promoting active participation by the society in achieving the objectives of existing national security and defense policies; guaranteeing the full operating capacity of the Armed Forces and the National Police, together with the system of national intelligence, all oriented to deterrence, defense of internal order, citizen security, prevention of conflicts and threats, and the maintenance of peace and regional security; fortifying civil-military relations; creating awareness of and fostering an understanding of the basic concepts of security and national defense in the educational system; and, finally, crafting the institutionalization of the Armed Forces and police forces, as well as the secret services.

In this context, the Peruvian population has a very valuable sociocultural potential which will permit constructing a vigorous culture of security and intelligence in the near future and which, together with an improving economy, will permit greater inclusiveness and social equality. The strategy which permitted the military-strategic defeat of the terrorist groups Sendero Luminoso (SL) and Túpac Amaru Revolutionary Movement (MRTA)—after a decade of subversive advances[53]—was sustained as part of a "new social contract" between the State, the forces of order, and the rural population. Peasant groups and self-defense committees[54] joined with the urban population (citizens who assisted the forces of order with information and mobilization

---

52 See *Libro Blanco de la Defensa Nacional del Perú*, April 2005, with a prologue by Minister of Defense Roberto Chiabra León, who notes that "on 9 September 2002, through Supreme Decree No. 009/SG, it was ordered that the White Book of National Defense be prepared by the Minister of Defense, in coordination with the Minister of Foreign Affairs and with the participation of the institutions responsible for security and national defense, other public authorities and sectors of society. The State policy for national defense was approved in March 2004 by the National Defense Council."

53 See *Conclusiones del informe final de la Comisión de la Verdad y Reconciliación (CVR), Chapter II: sobre el Partido Comunista del Perú-Sendero Luminoso (PCP-SL)*. The CVR says "the PCP-SL was the principal perpetrator of crimes and violations of human rights, taking as a measure of this the number of persons dead and disappeared. It was responsible for 54% of the fatal victims reported to the CVR." And among the conclusions regarding the responsibility of the apparatuses of the State, the CVR asserted that "the armed forces were capable of extracting lessons during the process of violence, which permitted refining their strategy in a way that would be more efficient and less disposed to massive violation of human rights. This lesson was revealed ostensibly in the decline of victims by the action of agents of the State precisely in the most intense years of armed internal conflict (1989-1993), while during these same years the PCP-SL manifested frantic terrorist violence toward the proliferation of the Self-Defense Committees, the operative police intelligence, and the backing of the citizenry, all of which explain the defeat of the PCP-SL."

54 From an ethnographic perspective, the history of the "rondas" (peasant patrols) and the self-defense committees are presented in Orin Starn, *Nightwatch: The Politics of Protest in the Andes* (Durham, NC: Duke University Press, 1999) (and additional, in Spanish).

to repudiate terrorism), isolating the subversives and undermining the backing they did have in the population.

This success was made possible by emphasizing operational and strategic intelligence, but also—and in contrast with the decade of the 1980s[55]—the Armed Forces and the National Police closed ranks with the poorer sectors of the population, looking to gain its support through humanitarian assistance, social assistance and the provision of security, rather than through the indiscriminate use of force. In this sense, it is worth remembering that on 5 July 1992 the chief of the Counterterrorism Directorate of Peru (DINCOTE) explained the strategy for combating terrorism and insurgency in the following terms:[56]

> *Intelligence in this fight is of the highest importance. The objective is to dismantle the organic apparatuses of the adversary and logically the first thing there is to do is to determine who they are, how they are organized, how they function; and the most effective and correct way to accomplish this is with intelligence. In that sense, we can say, without fear of equivocating, that at least in the military sphere, this is a war of intelligence, in which he who makes best use of it will advance. This year, complying with the directives of the Minister of the Interior and of the command of the National Police, we have introduced some substantial changes not only in the organic structure of the DINCOTE but also in its operating methodology. We can say that we are moving into an operational phase in which the work of intelligence is central, and is complemented with police investigative techniques.*

Using this approach, the DINCOTE, through the Special Intelligence Group (GEIN), captured the SL leader Abimael Guzmán and its leadership,

---

55 See also *Informe final de la CVR.. Volume II: los actores del conflicto, Chapter I. The armed forces 1.3.3.4.4. Del enfrentamiento con el legislativo al golpe de Estado de 1992*, where it is affirmed: "The Directive of the Ministry of Defense (003-91-MD/SDN), referring to the policy of pacification, developed in 1991 by the National Defense Secretariat, contains a broad political program that involved the military and non-military fields of Defense." Moreover, the CVR details that: "The same directive, in its Annex 01, makes an extraordinary critique of militarization" (of the counter-subversive process of the decade of the 1980s), expressing: "The non-application of the global anti-subversive strategy and the tendencies leading to a militarization, which narrows the resources of democracy, exposes the population to situations violating human rights. This situation ought to be addressed by the Constitution and laws of the State; the State is not able to concur in acts which delegitimize it. The crime of genocide is inherent to terrorist violence. Democracy is not able to respond with the same instruments and this is why it is necessary politically that the State and its forces of order be capable of protecting and respecting the lives of citizens."

56 See interview with General Antonio Ketín Vidal (who headed the DINCOTE during the capture of Abimael Guzmán), where he expounds on the strategy applied in defeating terrorism in Peru, which depended greatly on Intelligence and respecting human rights. Television program "La Ventana Indiscreta," channel 2, Lima, 19 Dec 2007. Available at: *http://agencia-peru.tv/ventana/?q--node/154.*

while the Second Intelligence Division dismantled the MRTA's planning cell without using violence nor violating human rights. In parallel fashion, in a joint effort with the Armed Forces, the SL was driven from the countryside to the city, leading to the imprisonment of nearly all its leaders and thousands of its followers, many of whom took advantage of the Amnesty Law to identify other members of the secretive organization.

This historic experience in defeating a growing terrorist threat, which had called into question the survival of Peru as a Nation-State,[57] certainly gives evidence of fertile terrain for the growth of a culture of security and intelligence, and the value of an anti-terrorist strategy which brought together various segments of this Andean country in an alliance to overcome mutual suspicions.

It cannot be denied that there were unfortunate excesses in the fight against terrorism, but this never formed part of the national strategy, nor was it part of the policy of the State, backed by the population. There were some isolated actions in the Valley of Mantaro and also the egregious crimes of Barrios Altos and La Cantuta in Lima.[58] The Peruvian Judiciary will determine if there was a secret plan to apply a supposed "dirty or clandestine war" contrary to human rights; but in retrospect these actions ended up being extraneous to the essential course of the winning strategy.[59]

As indicated by Andrés Gómez de la Torre and Alberto Bolívar, after failed efforts, debasement, and perversion of the system or through simple ineptitude, the Peruvian intelligence system was reduced practically to ashes by the actions of autocrats as well as by democrats. In the wake of the abuses committed by national intelligence in the decade of the 1990s, due to a distorted perception of the importance of national security, intermingled with irresponsible

---

57 See Santiago Roncagliolo, *La cuarta espada. La historia de Abimael Guzmán y Sendero Luminoso*, First Edition (Argentina: Editorial Sudamericana, 2007), pp. 140-141, 160-161.

58 A paramilitary detachment called "Colina" was accused by the Justice Ministry of having executed extrajudicially 15 persons on the grounds of Barrios Altos in the center of Lima (1991), and nine students and a professor of the University of La Cantuta, also in Lima (1992). See also Ricardo Uceda, *Muerte en el Pentagonito*, First Edition (Bogota: Editorial Planeta Colombiana, 2004), p. 290, where the author indicates: "This account, which has gained great force, has yet to be tested judicially. A more elaborate account is developed in the report of the CVR, (1.3.4.3, The special operations of the National Intelligence Service-SIN), according to which the Colina Group was directed by the SIN, employing inteligence personnel who acted on the margin of their official chain of command." See also, regarding this particular issue, "Condenan a 35 años de cárcel al ex jefe del SIN," daily *El Comercio*, Lima, 4 Sep 2008 – Primera Planta, where it is reported that a general of the Army in retirement, former chief of SIN, was sentenced on 4 Aug 2008 to 35 years in prison for the kidnapping and deaths of nine students and one professor of the University of La Cantuta. The First Anti-corruption Court in addition sentenced former members of the Colina Group to 15 years in prison for the same crime.

59 See also "La estrategia ganadora" by Jaime de Althaus, daily *El Comercio*, 14 Dec 2007. Althaus is an anthropologist, journalist, and writer, and author of the book: *La revolución capitalista en el Perú* (Fondo de Cultura Económica, 2007).

political reprisal, at the beginning of the last six-year period (2001-2006), the budget for national defense diminished drastically, and a process of restructuring was forced on the Armed Forces and, by extension, onto the national intelligence community.[60]

Despite a strong democratic consensus and what Alberto Bolivar labels "politically correct" rhetoric, neither the transition regime of president Valentín Paniagua (November 2000-July 2001)[61] nor the five-year term of Alejandro Toledo (July 2001- July 2006), proved capable of putting in place a national intelligence system suitable for the security needs of the country and the region.[62] Both Peruvian authors describe the decline in the country's intelligence services in this period, agreeing that a cultural predilection toward informality and permissiveness contributed to fragile intelligence institutions with a low degree of professionalism and weak operational efficiency.[63] In the failed attempt to reconstruct the intelligence system, in addition to dismissing real criminals who had infiltrated the system, a large number of true, specialized intelligence professionals were also dismissed.

Damage Control in the DINI?

This situation has not been corrected, due to resistance from some of the management of the current National Directorate of Intelligence (DINI). As the DINI does not have available to it personnel who are well-versed in strategic intelligence, save the half-dozen analysts who survived the indiscriminate dismissals of the past six-year period, plus a small group of professionals who joined the service in the chaotic period of the CNI, it would not be prudent to commit these individuals immediately to purely strategic analysis. What can be done, without losing a strategic and global vision, is to opt for the integration of intelligence specialists who focus on internal problems in

---

60 See also "Pronto FFAA repararán su propio armamento. Paniagua redujo inversions miiitares del 20 al 5 por ciento," the daily *Expreso*, Political Section, Lima, 6 Dec 2007.

61 At the end of the transition government of President Valentín Paniagua—elected after the Fujimori administration collapsed—the Congress of the Republic promulgated in June 2001 law No. 27479, which created a new National Intelligence System (SINA), with the National Intelligence Council (CNI) providing oversight.

62 See articles by Jorge Serrano Torres on the Red Voltaire-France and the IPI Agency Web sites: "La reconstrucción del sistema de inteligencia peruano" (11 Jul 2006); "Servicio secreto: ¿espionaje político y corrupción?" (24 Aug 2005) and "Destrucción del sistema de inteligencia peruano" (14 Sep 2004). Available at *http://www.voltairenet.org./auteur4574.html?lang=es*.

63 There is consensus among Peruvian analysts regarding the following: an icon for the incompetence of the CNI is the case of a chief of counterintelligence who, during the directorship of retired general Daniel Mora, was taped, filmed, and photographed while plotting against the Minister of the Interior of the Peruvian government. See "CNI conspires against Minister Rospigliosi," pp. 2 and 3, daily newspaper *Correo* of Lima, 18 Mar 2004.

Peru with those who would be analysts of foreign issues. They would together identify the factors driving change and evolution in the region.[64]

Among other things, they could analyze a series of hypotheses of low probability, which nevertheless need to be taken into account, for the great potential impact they could have—the so-called "low probability-high impact" scenarios. Also, they could identify heretofore unanticipated and imponderable phenomena, or "wild cards,"[65] of high potential impact. The difference between the first and second is that the latter involve issues which the region cannot control nor avoid.

Another issue addressed by Andres Gomez and Alberto Bolivar is the absence of a strong academic environment for the promotion of a culture of security and intelligence in Peru. One cannot count on a serious academic, intellectual debate on the importance of strategic intelligence in the country. Also lacking are specialized periodical publications, such as a journal that could be produced under the auspices of the National Intelligence School, like those in Spain, Argentina, and Brazil. Such publications help to generate a culture of intelligence whereby the citizenry understands the function of the secret services—complete with its myths and toxic prejudices—and learns that the intelligence function is a key piece of State infrastructure in its guaranteeing general security and the stability of the democratic system.

Peruvians should have confidence that the intelligence services operate with absolute respect for the Rule of Law, and observe regulations and well-defined political, legal, and judicial controls. For that reason, it should be noted that some private-sector educational institutions do present academic intelligence studies programs. Among them are those of Strategos, the Institute of Intelligence Analysis and Dissemination, led by Alberto Bolívar, and another program managed by the Mariátegui Chair of Political and Strategic Studies, in association with the University Ricardo Palma of Lima, both of which offer certificates in Intelligence and Counterintelligence; Security, Policy, and Strategy; as well as Strategic Studies in the Regional grouping of Peru-Chile-Bolivia. Prospectively, a Master's in Political and Strategic Studies will be offered.

The Value of Human Intelligence

As the Peruvian authors here point out, the typical approach in the country has been for either civilian or military agencies to apply archaic,

---

64 The term "drivers" of change is developed in *Latinoamérica 2020: Pensando los Escenarios de Largo Plazo*, proceedings of a seminar held in Santiago, Chile, 7-8 June 2004, within the framework of the *Global Trends Project 2020* of the National Intelligence Council of the U.S.

65 *Latinoamérica 2020: Pensando los Escenarios de Largo Plazo*, ibid.

monopolistic practices to intelligence. Common sense would indicate that intelligence requires multi-agency, multi-disciplinary work and rigorous methodology, where the intelligence professional systematically challenges conventional thinking, developing alternatives and scenarios to maximize the use of imagination, engages in careful study, and applies skill, experience, and ethical awareness within the framework of a somewhat mystical, patriotic theology.

Viable professionalism in intelligence will not result from addressing the struggle for primacy between the civilians and the military, but from overcoming the problem of having unsuitable or incapable professionals conduct the specialized work of intelligence. To attract and retain the best human resources, there needs to be a promising work environment where officials work for the State and not primarily for the successive governments. Such ideal employees could be civilian or military.

In the intelligence crisis of 2001, both civilian and military personnel were dismissed on a massive scale,[66] creating a vacuum in the realm of strategic intelligence analysis that has yet to be filled.[67] On the contrary, the DIGIMIN (the General Intelligence Directorate of the Ministry of the Interior), along with the Intelligence Directorate, the Antidrug Directorate, and the Counterterrorism Directorate of the National Police,[68] had the foresight and the responsibility to keep their personnel, and even to recover those police agents and analysts who were in the "formal SIN" and those who had been sent into retirement arbitrarily.[69] This was something that did not occur either in the CNI or in military intelligence.

---

66 See *Ideele* (magazine of the Institute of Legal Defense) interview in 2001 of the then-first chief of the CNI, retired Admiral Alfonzo Panizo, who in addressing the question, "How have you deactivated the famous SIN of the Fujimori and Montesinos era?" responded: "Totally, in the era of Montesinos there had been what could be called a real, effective, and efficient SIN; and a false SIN, which utilized the elements of intelligence to benefit a clique and not to benefit the country." Despite this development, nearly all of the personnel of the ex-SIN departed, both those culpable and those innocent. Please see *http://www.idl.org.pe/idlrev/revistas/142/pag55.htm*.

67 See "Un mini-sistema de inteligencia en lugar de nada," p. A-6, in the daily newspaper *El Comercio*, 12 September 2007, where it was affirmed: "It has been more than a decade that we know and feel that we do not have a system of national intelligence. And the worst part is that we the governing and those who are governed live believing that we have one."

68 See "Reivindican al policia que desactivó el MRTA," daily newspaper *La Razón*, Lima, p. 5, 9 December 2007, where it is mentioned that after his having been moved into retirement unjustly in 2001, General Juan Gonzales Sandoval was decorated by the National Police in the Ministry of Interior due to his prominent role in the fight against terrorism.

69 See "El Operativo Volcán en Cerro Azul," *Boletín del Instituto de Defensa Legal* (IDL), 28 November 2007, which highlights the successful work of operational intelligence, which, through combined teams from DINCOTE and the Special Operations Directorate of the National Police, located, captured, or brought down terrorist kingpins of Sendero Luminoso. Also see "Los que vuelven a la Policía Nacional," Department of Citizen Security of IDL, 23 November 2007, which tells the story of an experienced chief of counterintelligence who returned to investigatory tasks with the National Police.

It remains clear, consequently, that the greater importance accorded the DIGIMIN, compared to DINI, is not because of any incompetence or lack of leadership of the chiefs of the latter entity, but rather that the DIGIMIN has exhibited a greater operational capacity through the experience and continuity of its personnel, that is to say, of its human resources, including its chief. The DIGIMIN has been especially useful to Executive Branch decisionmakers in their handling of internal security.[70] Therefore, in place of continuing inter-agency disagreements, an alternative is to have the chief of the DINI, as the official with highest rank in the National Intelligence System (SINA), and with the knowledge of the Prime Minister and of the President of the Republic, formulate plans for improving interoperability between intelligence central— DINI—and the secret police and military services which comprise the SINA, notwithstanding the continuing need for some legal reform involving the Intelligence Committee of Congress.

Identification of Threats for Peru

The Peruvian *Libro Blanco* (White Book) of National Defense[71] identifies as external threats 1) those which may be generated in the South American sub-region through the application of incompatible security doctrines; 2) those which can arise from a crisis related to the scarcity of natural resources of strategic value (including water or gas supply, for example); as well as 3) terrorism, drug trafficking, and international crime. Among internal threats are those groups which, contrary to constitutional order, opt for violence; radical groups which promote social violence and popular uprising; common but organized crime; illicit traffic of drugs; corruption and the destruction of the environment.[72]

In this framework, the fragility of Peruvian intelligence acquires meaning in external terms, given that an effective international strategy against such phenomena as terrorism, drug trafficking, or international organized crime,

---

70 See "Cambios, movidas en el Mininter," *Instituto de Defensa Legal*-IDL, 1 February 2008 (*http://seguridadidl.org/pe/boletin/2008/01-02.htm*), which notes, "From the fall of the dictatorship, the DIGIMIN was converted into the only system of intelligence which provided more or less reliable information to the diverse sectors hungry for intelligence, among those the Palace of Government.

71 See *Libro Blanco de la Defensa Nacional del Perú*, Chapter III, Política de Estado para la Seguridad y la Defensa Nacional: Identificación de Amenazas, 15 April 2005. Available at http://www.mindef.gob.pe/.

72 To be certain, one must note the worldwide threat represented by Climatic Change or Global Warming, which is already affecting the Amazon watershed and the glaciers of Peru. See Ban Ki-moon, Secretary General of the UN, "El Liderazgo y el Cambio Climático," Web site of the UN in Peru, December 2007. Similarly, see *Una verdad incómoda (An Inconvenient Truth)*, narrated by Al Gore, ex-Vice President of the U.S. and 2007 Nobel Peace Prize winner.

which have metastasized, depends on a diligent collaboration among States. As manifested by Michael Herman of St. Antony's College of Oxford, even a super-power such as the U.S. is unable to provide the intelligence necessary for its own national security using only its own resources. The globalized world needs greater inter-governmental collaboration,[73] but for that to occur governments must build better intelligence services.

The Chavista-Cuban Danger in the Region and the Need for a Culture of Security and National Intelligence

Andres Gomez de la Torre suggests that the political divisions among the countries of South America, which have broken free of old geopolitical systems and alliances, "will complicate the desirable and necessary cooperation and coordination needed to confront common threats." He refers to the activities of Venezuela's Chavez administration, which many security and intelligence organizations and governmental elites of the region are not prepared to confront, do not understand, or are reluctant to recognize. This situation reflects the absence, in a majority of the countries of the region, of a solid national security and intelligence culture.[74]

And despite the fact that the Venezuelan president suffered a defeat in December 2007,[75] when he attempted to modify the Constitution in order to establish a regime which would have allowed his indefinite continuation in power as a messianic leader, his regional ambitions remain viable, given his tight alliance with Cuba.[76]

---

[73] Preface by Michael Herman in Russell G. Swenson and Susana C. Lemozy, Editors/ Compilers, *Intelligence Professionalism in the Americas* (Washington, DC, 2004), available at *http://www.ndic.edu/press/6921.htm.*

[74] See Jorge Serrano Torres, "Hugo Chávez Frías: perfíl y estrategia de gobierno," Web page of Diario Atajo y Avizora de Argentina, November 2007, available at *http://www.avizora. com/atajo/colaboradores/textos_jorge_serrano_torres/0010_chavez-perfíl_estrategia_gobierno. htm.* Similarly: "Venezuela: perfíl de Hugo Chávez y su estrategia espansionista," *AAinteligencia*, March 2008, available at *http://www.aainteligencia.cl/2008/Mar2008_3_JorgeSerrano.html.*

[75] See "'No pudimos ... por ahora'; acepta Hugo Chávez derrota en el referendo," daily *La Jornada*-Mexico, 3 December 2007.

[76] See "Firman Raúl Castro y Hugo Chávez acuerdos por cientos de millones de dólares," daily newspaper *La Jornada*, Mexico D.F., *Sección Mundo*, 16 October 2007, where the following is reported: "the president of Venezuela insists in one of his proposals to the Cubans: 'We will be able in the near future to create a confederation of republics; two republics into one, two countries into one.'" The ties between the regime of Chavez and Cuba are found at all levels: the state business Telecom Venezuela and the Cuban company Transbit, with the aid of China Popular, will lay a submarine fiber optic cable 1,552 kilometers long at a cost of $70 million U.S., which will unite La Guajira in the north of Venezuela and Ciboney in the province of Santiago de Cuba. This infrastructure project, in addition to empowering Cuban Internet communications, implements control over the national and external communications of the persons and institutions hostile to the Chavez regime, under the guidance of the Cuban counterintelligence service.

The Venezuelan regime employs a "three-legged Diplomacy": through State-to-State relations; in the Economic-Energy sector (advantageous investments or subsidies); and by direct, personal interaction with political leaders, as well as with Latin American social and business partners. He is supported by the General Directorate of Military Intelligence (DGIM), whose chief is the strongman of Venezuelan intelligence and of Chavez's "Praetorian Guard,"[77] which is being modernized and systematically strengthened.[78]

Chavez's advances are not exempt from stumbles: His campaign for a strong policy against dissent was derailed when, in June 2008, he agreed to abandon a new National Intelligence and Counterintelligence Law, which was in effect for only 13 days,[79] leaving its fate in the hands of the National Parliament for eventual discussion and reform. The aborted law violated human rights and the constitution in decreeing that Venezuelans and foreigners, if they refused to cooperate with his intelligence agencies as informants, could be jailed for up to four years.

A Possible Course of Action on the Basis of Compared Experience

Considering the influence of culture in the functioning of the national intelligence services, the experience resulting from analyzing the evolution (or in some cases the deterioration) of the secret services of Mexico, Venezuela, Colombia, Ecuador, Brazil, Argentina, Chile, Guatemala, the U.S., Russia, and Peru[80] shows that, in instances of institutional crisis, no country is able to disassemble completely its national intelligence center—as occurred in Peru—

---

77 See "El Montesinos de Chávez," *Semana* magazine, Colombia, number 1344, 2 February 2008.

78 See Jorge Serrano Torres, "El sistema de inteligencia venezolano y la Guerra asimétrica." Original source: Voltairenet.org., published in *el Portal de Noticias de Información de Defensa* (Spain), 13 December 2005. Available at http://foroplus.net/noticias/getnewsitem. php?newsid=1693.

79 See "Henry Rangel Silva: Nueva ley de inteligencia se concibe para la seguridad de todo el Estado," Web page of *Venezolana de Televisión*, Caracas, 4 June 2008. Also see "Chávez deroga ley de inteligencia," CNNEXPANSION.com. (Caracas-Reuters), 10 June 2008. It is pertinent to note that the Venezuelan intelligence reform initiative created four specialized institutions: the General Directorate of Intelligence and the General Directorate of Counterintelligence, assigned to the Ministry of the Interior; and the General Directorate of Military Intelligence and the General Directorate of Military Counterintelligence, dependent on the Ministry of Defense. Following the model and advice of Cuban intelligence, these changes responded to the necessity to create new and more powerful secret services, in order to replace the current ones, with the end of confronting supposed interference by the U.S. in internal Venezuelan affairs, along with shoring up the intelligence activities of the Chavez government in the region.

80 See Carlos Maldonado Prieto, *Servicios de Inteligencia en Sudamérica: Estado de situación en una perspective comparada* (Fort Benning, Georgia: Western Hemisphere Institute for Security Cooperation, 2002).

without placing both its internal and external intelligence services in a state of serious vulnerability.[81] In this way, the Peruvian case is projected as an anti-model which ought not to be carried out in an intelligence system that undergoes a deep crisis and suffers a loss of legitimacy.

What's more, one can infer that during a process of "restructuring," "reengineering," "refunding," "reconstruction," "modernization" (or whatever it may be called) of a system of intelligence, the most prudent approach is to carry out a thorough cleansing of the system through a counterintelligence initiative to destroy only the noxious and unserviceable elements, rather than trying to return to "Year Zero."[82] Most importantly, it costs a lot in money, time, and effort to recruit and train intelligence personnel and get them adapted successfully to organizational culture and institutional idiosyncrasies, not to mention the intelligence work itself. This is even more true for a country in which the culture of national security and intelligence has not taken root or has deteriorated.

For a country where intelligence has been implicated in the violation of human rights, political espionage, and corruption, the most practical approach would be to remove only the highest level of officials, keeping the next lower level of managers, the most capable, experienced, and efficient who are not tainted. The ultimate aim is to have "serious but invisible middle managers" that make an organization operate smoothly, like the distributor in a car: vital to its operation, but remaining unnoticed until it ceases to function.[83]

In an essay in this book, Joanisval Brito Goncalves describes what occurred during the failed Brazilian government of Fernando Collor de Mello in March 1990, with the decreed extinction of the controversial and powerful National Information Service (SNI). In the Brazilian case—as distinct from the Peruvian one—military and police intelligence not only were maintained, but were strengthened, when the national intelligence center disappeared. This leads one to believe that the painful period through which Brazilian intelligence passed is being fully overcome, even in a place where there remains considerable tension between the intelligence community and the political class, thanks to the Lula da Silva administration's betting on the robust institutions

---

81 See essays regarding the secret services of Peru, Chile, Argentina, Brazil, Ecuador, Colombia, Venezuela, Guatemala, Mexico, U.S., and Russia, published by Jorge Serrano Torres, in Red Voltaire, available at *http://www.voltairenet.org/auteur4574.html?lang=es*.

82 "Año Cero": Term utilized by the genocidal Khmer Rouge of Cambodia in the 1970s for announcing the complete destruction of all that was not linked directly to the Communist Party—with the intention of reconstructing it afterward from "nothing."

83 See also Bob Woodward, *Negar la evidencia: Bush en Guerra, parte III* (Bogota: Grupo Editorial Norma, 2006), p. 122. In English, it carries the title, *State of Denial: Bush at War, Part III* (New York: Simon and Schuster, 2006).

and professionalism of the intelligence establishment. As a result, its national intelligence system is perceived as one of the more efficient and developed in all the region.[84]

A Look at Mexican National Intelligence and National Culture

A similar, destructive approach to handling human resources occurred in Mexico during the transition of power from the Institutional Revolutionary Party (PRI) to the Fox administration at the end of 2000. One result was that the chief intelligence institution, the National Security Research Center (CISEN), was unable to warn about the terrorism attacks perpetrated by the People's Revolutionary Army (EPR) against the national oil company (PEMEX) in September 2007.[85] In the aftermath, the Chief of the Government Department had to explain to the Chamber of Deputies of the Congress that more than 1,000 CISEN professionals had been removed from their posts in recent years. He attributed this failure by CISEN to the simultaneous reduction in funding it had suffered. The administration of Felipe Calderón has taken the decision to increase CISEN's personnel numbers and to modernize its infrastructure.[86]

Without denying the weakened capability of CISEN, the Mexican observer Manuel Balcázar Villarreal finds that a national intelligence culture is already in formation, thanks to greater institutional confidence and improved professionalism in intelligence. This advancement permits national intelligence organizations, as well as emissaries from private enterprise, to build stronger cooperative links with foreign counterparts, with respect to transnational threats.

Balcázar applauds the separation of analytic and operational functions in CISEN. In his judgment, this brings greater efficiency to both areas. At the same time, he sees the need to achieve greater coordination between operations and analysis. The author also recommends greater interaction between intelligence leaders and national communications media to overcome the perils of too much secrecy and a resultant ostracism by the Mexican public.

---

84 Dos de los últimos jefes de la Abin en el gobierno de Lula han sido funcionarios de inteligencia de carrera: la psicóloga Marisa Del'Isola Diniz, funcionaria que ha trabajado casi 30 años en actividades de inteligencia, habiendo sido responsable—durante siete años—de la oficina de Formación de Recursos Humanos del Servicio Nacional de Informaciones (durante el gobierno militar). Otro jefe de la Abin fue Marcio Paulo Buzanelli, quien tiene el rango de Comandante de Inteligencia y una experiencia y continuidad de 29 años en el sistema de inteligencia brasilero.

85 Cfr. Artículo: "Sumergido en su crisis sigue el Cisen: Cataño Contreras," página Web *La Prensa-OEM*. México, 20 January 2008.

86 Cfr. Artículos: "Fallas del Cisen evitaron prever ataques del EPR," diario *El Mañana* de México, 26/09/2007. Y "Crea Segob 200 plazas nuevas para el Cisen," diario *El Universal* de México, 28 November 2007.

After all, as in many other countries, the intelligence services in Mexico were employed as political police during the hegemonic regime that ruled the country for several decades.

The author goes on to note that his own study of Mexican intelligence institutions, based on simple organizational diagrams of successive intelligence entities, has been enriched by information available in press reports, although much official information remains restricted despite the somewhat greater openness in recent years.

A Revealing Glimpse of Colombian National Intelligence

In contrast to developments in Peru and Mexico, when in October 2005 the central intelligence institution in Colombia, the DAS (Administrative Department of Security), was at the center of an intelligence scandal, the Colombian government did not dismantle the DAS through massive and indiscriminate layoffs. Instead, the outcome was that the chief of DAS was jailed and the deputy chief sacked, and the organization underwent a significant reorganization, as directed by the Uribe administration.[87] A government commission oversaw internal investigations that subjected 1,646 officials to the polygraph, of whom 273 were subjected to further questioning, leading in the end to the dismissal of 106 officials.[88] Under the theme of "zero tolerance for corruption," these individuals were separated without generating a rupture or great institutional upheaval in the DAS.[89]

This background allows a greater appreciation of the essay by Vicente Torrijos of Colombia. He explains that the keys to understanding national intelligence in his country are the multiple and interconnected threats—narcotrafficking, insurgents, paramilitaries, and organized scofflaws—that have generated a corresponding intelligence culture accustomed to diversity, aware of the need to conduct systematic analyses, and chiefly, one that is receptive to education that thereby builds institutional capital. However, the author remains uneasy about an incomplete institutional structure in the intelligence services that restrains a fuller development of an intelligence culture. The fragmented nature of the intelligence community is abetted by the frequent public confrontations between the leadership of DAS and of military intelligence in recent years. Additionally,

40 |

---

87 Cfr. Artículo: "DAS-Gate: la detención de Jorge Noguera, ex director del DAS, deja tres preguntas: por qué el presidente lo nombró, por qué duró tanto y por qué lo defendió," versión Web de la Revista *Semana* de Colombia, 24 February2007.

88 Cfr. "En qué anda el DAS," página Web de la revista *Semana*, Sección Nación, 24 February 2007.

89 Cfr. "El director del DAS anuncia que el organismo será sometido a una completa reorganización," *Europa Press*, 04 November 2005.

as in several other countries of the region, both civilian and military intelligence leaders have experienced a rapid rotation in and out of their positions. Leadership of the intelligence services seems to be a step in a career ladder rather than a long-term commitment. This problem also does not promote the maturation of a "corporate culture" within the principal agencies.

Torrijos does not pass up the opportunity to point out that the Colombian intelligence apparatus—its paradigms and procedures—is based primarily on a military model. Paraphrasing Georges Clemenceau, who during World War I commented that "war is too important to leave in the hands of the military," so Torrijos suggests that "intelligence is too complex a phenomenon to reduce it to its military dimensions." He emphasizes that intelligence is at base a political instrument.

Cultural Influences in Argentine Intelligence

The distinguished Argentine essayist, José Manuel Ugarte, asks an intriguing question: Can a country's cultural inheritances be surmounted? At length, his answer is that, just as Argentina and other countries in Latin America have taken several steps toward institutionalizing democracy, so can and should their intelligence services become more legitimate and effective.

After an extensive and critical historical analysis of the Argentine case, Ugarte points out that a key criterion indicating progress toward that goal would find intelligence professionals and their organizations replacing their loyalty to political personalities and to successive governments with a deeper sense of service to the nation. Some of the signals of that progress would be: improving their technical capability, giving priority to the analytic function, careful husbanding of operating funds, and ensuring that intelligence protect both the state and the citizens from threats, thereby gaining for intelligence the needed prestige and social recognition.

Finally, Ugarte tries to relieve some of his own concerns about the intelligence services in his own country by reminding us that Argentina is not alone in this struggle. He suggests that the continual complaints voiced about intelligence services across the region allow us to infer that at least in some Latin American countries, intelligence services do play a significant role in the political sphere. This observation suggests, in turn, the ever-present risk that national governments can "kill liberty in the name of security," which is also the title of an article by Oxford University professor Timothy Garton Ash[90]

---

90 Timothy Garton Ash, Professor of Contemporary History at Oxford University, "Matar la libertad en nombre de la seguridad," *El Comercio* newspaper, p. b-4, 25 November 2007.

Another author from Argentina, Jorge Osvaldo Sillone, makes it clear that, in his country, many aspects of the intelligence services have their origin in the experience of the armed forces as national, founding institutions. The armed forces have long been responsible to warn of threats to society. Now, he finds that civilians are full participants in national, strategic intelligence circles. Thus, when it is appropriate to blame intelligence for a strategic mistake, that blame can be placed on the entire culture of the society, rather than only on military organizations.

Sillone also argues that what remains unremarked about the world situation today, in contrast with earlier historical periods, is that no country can unilaterally declare itself "neutral" with respect to threats from international terrorism for the simple reason that this type of violence does not have a clear cause nor a recognized nation that assumes responsibility. He adds that to unravel the threads of this conflict locally, regionally, and worldwide, remains the great challenge for strategic intelligence. He recommends greater international cooperation to address this challenge.

A third Argentinean essayist, Heriberto Justo Auel, presents interesting philosophical reflections on the complex relationship between the culture of the country and its leaders, on the one hand, and the phenomenon of strategic intelligence on the other. He charges that the "system of strategic intelligence" has since the 1980s been legally paralyzed and continues in a downward spiral, having lost a good part of its social capital and in addition being subjected to a retributive intelligence law that makes it less than viable. He suggests that those who doubt this criticism only need to objectively compare Argentine reality with the rules that regulate the security, defense, and intelligence institutions. He adds that the country suffers from laws that are clearly anti-institutional, that prevent thinking about the future, and that are leading inexorably toward "legal improvisation." These factors are leading Argentina to be a "failed state," unable to counter non-state enemies.

In a caustic manner, Auel condemns the existence of a "tolerant, secular society" in the West which "hates itself" so much that it tries to confront non-state enemies as if we were not already at war; that is, by negotiating and applying a civilian penal code to soldiers to "protect the rights of our enemies." To highlight the obligation of the intelligence services in Argentina and elsewhere, he quotes Ezekiel 33:6:

> *If the watchman sees the sword coming and does not blow the trumpet to warn the people, and the sword comes and takes the life of one of them, that man will be taken away because of his sin, but I will hold the watchman accountable.*

To conclude his observations, Auel gives us to understand that the "sentinel" of Latin American states is the remnant "quasi-Ibero-American nation-state," which, if not reinvigorated and made capable of sounding the horn—which we know to be the function of strategic intelligence—so that it can be heard in time to confront the new threat and defeat it, then it will have abandoned its role as essential complement to national culture.

Limitations and Challenges of Canadian National Culture and the Canadian Intelligence Services

As a contrast to the essay in this book that compares Brazilian and Canadian intelligence services in the context of their national cultures, Stephane Lefebvre contributes a separate essay on Canadian intelligence services. With a critical eye, he notes that Canadian intelligence habitually has played only a marginal role in decision making by political leaders and even high-level, career government officials, to include the diplomatic corps.

He argues that intelligence gains attention in Canada only in cases of scandalous activity. This he attributes to the absence of a critical mass of civilian specialists in security and intelligence, as well as the failure of mass media which could explain in meaningful terms the value of national intelligence. He also assigns blame to the lack of a national intelligence strategy and the corresponding lack of a long-term view of intelligence in the national enterprise, which would value the development of intelligence scenarios related to Canadian national interests.

Lefebvre is convinced that whereas the strategic culture of Canada does not recognize intelligence as part of the matrix of Canadian national power, the growth of an intelligence-oriented culture beyond that obtaining among intelligence practitioners themselves remains in doubt. Nonetheless, the author admits that, despite an erosion of intelligence capabilities prior to 9/11, after that date Canadian intelligence has been reorganized, fortified with increased resources, including both civilian and military personnel, and has even experienced an improvement in its public image.

The author suggests that Canada's political leaders were surprised by the events of 9/11, not having paid attention to the Canadian Security Intelligence Service's (CSIS) detailed assessments that were available about the threat of global terrorism, and specifically about Al Qaeda. Most parliamentarians in the country also hold only a superficial understanding of intelligence. Again, it is only when an intelligence scandal erupts that this government function is discussed. One avenue toward improving this state of affairs is through the educational system. However, by the author's calculation, of the 79 universities in Canada, a total of only nine courses are offered that are clearly related to intelligence.

A few positive signs now appear on the horizon. Canadian intelligence agencies do not operate outside the law, as each has a legislative base for its activities. Further, although the country's identity is in constant flux, strong ties of cooperation are maintained, by all of the intelligence agencies, with allies like the U.S., the UK, Australia, and New Zealand. Although Canadian experts for more than a decade have fought for the creation of a foreign intelligence agency with a focus outside the country, which is beyond the purview of the CSIS, this effort has not yet gained official backing.

Lefebvre makes an important distinction: even if no recognizable intelligence culture exists at the national level, a strong sub-culture does exist among practitioners in the intelligence community itself. This sub-culture rests on the professional foundation of a strong sense of secrecy, a dynamic relationship with intelligence communities in the Anglo-sphere, a separation of intelligence practice and police practice, and an acceptance of review and oversight by government bodies. Still, the development of a real, national intelligence culture awaits the day when intelligence is more formally integrated into the creation of national policies.

The Relationship between Culture and Intelligence in Brazil and Canada

The Brazilian author Joanisval Brito Gonçalves offers an interesting perspective, comparing the perceptions of Brazilians and Canadians about their respective intelligence services. Both countries are challenged to convince their population, including their leaders, that intelligence has great relevance to facing down organized crime and terrorism.

The author makes the very interesting observation that, in the turbulent years before the creation of the Brazilian Intelligence Agency (ABIN), several developed-country intelligence systems were evaluated as models for Brazil. The Canadian system was found to be the most appropriate fit, and it was adopted for the December 1999 inauguration of ABIN. However, he concludes that, in terms of intelligence transformation, and of its cultural acceptance, Canada has surpassed Brazil. A major difference is that, since its creation, the Canadian Security Intelligence Service (CSIS) has focused on demonstrating to the Canadian people its capacity to protect their security.

More specifically, Brito Gonçalves suggests that CSIS gained public credence from publishing a widely available report on strategic aspects of the Canadian economy. It allowed the public to understand the work of CSIS on behalf of the society. Notably, ABIN has followed the same path with its publication of the *Brazilian Intelligence Journal*, which aims to reveal to the public what it is that intelligence does. Both Canada and Brazil have increased public awareness of their activities by hosting open seminars, granting press interviews, and emphasizing their responsiveness to Congress. At the same time, an area where intelligence agencies need to be more responsive, particularly in Brazil, where any report of telephone tapping is automatically ascribed to the intelligence services, is in clearly rebutting such accusations.

Another service that intelligence organizations in both countries can offer is some tailored support to private enterprises about foreign operating risks, including foreign-origin industrial espionage. Intelligence services in both countries can be of value in areas of scientific and technical knowledge. Both countries host cutting-edge technology companies in nuclear, aerospace and biotech industries, and the intelligence services can play a major role in safeguarding these enterprises by raising industrialists' consciousness of security threats to them.

The CSIS, like ABIN, has taken steps to gain acceptance among young people, especially among those who might later join the intelligence services. Both services have brought students to visit their installations and have programs underway to maintain the interest of youths.

The Cultural Fabric of Brazilian Strategic Intelligence

The second Brazilian essayist, Glauco Moraes, agrees to some extent with his compatriot in thinking that, during the democratic florescence after 1990, the earlier actions of the powerful National Intelligence Service (SNI) engendered a public firestorm at the hands of those who were pursued and persecuted by the SNI, and who after 1990 were influential members of the political class in the new democratic era.

The author finds that this fierce prejudice against the intelligence services, along with the political problems generated during the military government, forged a national culture that was at odds with and actively resisted everything associated with national security and intelligence. He goes on to suggest that such antipathy, when it prevails, comes to emphasize form over substance and directly affects the functionality of national intelligence by tainting public service. A notable lesson from this episode is that when an intelligence service bows to bureaucratic pressure to achieve success at any cost, in the end the service is treated to negative cultural consequences.

Applying this important point to the real-world environment of global terrorism, including that associated with Islamic fundamentalism, we may infer that intelligence services must pay close attention to maintaining "proper form" even when they are tasked to come up with a quick resolution of a crisis to save innocent human lives. For example, when forced to apply physical and psychological pressure to obtain critical information through interrogation,[91] they must avoid "torture" of a terrorist cell member who is suspected of with-holding that information.[92] In a society with a tendency to favor form over sub-stance, this scenario harbors a very touchy issue for professional intelligence protagonists as well as for decision makers and the society itself, as it involves the human rights of terrorists as well as those of terrorist victims.[93]

At the same time, the author also notes that, especially among intellec-tuals in Brazil, an idea with considerable currency is that intelligence boils down to "spy games" that aim at societal control, secret funding, and targeting com-peting politicians, all within a culture that sees laws as a source of punishment rather than as a societal norm that needs to be taken into account at all times. He attributes such misunderstandings and distrust to a limited exposure of the intelligence voice in debates on defense issues. In Brazil, there has been practi-cally no education about the intelligence function outside of the military and the state security apparatus. Further, in those environments, technical training in intelligence rather than intelligence education has been the norm.

Nonetheless, the author remains optimistic, seeing that despite the pre-vailing difficulties, there is a real potential for the growth of a national intel-ligence culture. This optimism is warranted because the individuals from an older generation who were tainted with the intelligence excesses of the Cold War are now leaving their positions of power in the country. Other reasons for optimism: the increasing number of intelligence courses being offered in both public and private educational institutions, especially since 2001; better treat-ment of the field in recent years by the mass communications media; and the creation of some 200 intelligence units in diverse public institutions at federal, state, and municipal levels.

This improvement is abetted by still other factors. First is the sense that police intelligence at the national level needs to be improved to counter increased criminal activity and the corresponding dip in personal security among the population, especially in the larger cities. Additionally, the Brazil-ian Intelligence Agency (ABIN) itself is engaging in public outreach through,

91 See Gustavo Gorriti, "Tenet y el submarine," *Caretas* magazine, No. 1974, 5 March 2007, which questions the application of "enhanced interrogation techniques," as described by a high-level U.S. intelligence official, but who claimed such techniques do not constitute torture. Further, the official claimed that these techniques have "saved lives" in the period after 9/11.

92 See *Jerrold Pos*, "Identidad colectiva: el odio que se inculca desde los huesos," *eJournal USA*, electronic journal of the U.S. Department of State, May 2007. Available at *http://usinfo. state.gov/journals/itps/0507/ijps/post.htm.*

93 See *Mohammed M. Hafez*, "Caso de estudio: lo mítico del martirologio en Iraq", *eJour-nal USA*, May 2007. Available at *http://usinfo.state.gov/journals/itps/0507/ijps/hafez.htm.*

among other things, staging open competitions for the acquisition of new employees, although this practice carries some security risk. Since 2004, this agency has overcome its traditional practice of having "no comment" about accusations of impropriety or calls for greater openness. It now hosts public seminars, with international participation, on security issues. The author also finds that ABIN has improved its image through the publication of the *Brazilian Intelligence Journal*. All these actions have worked toward demystifying the country's intelligence establishment, with expectations of medium and long-term, positive results.

Evolution of Intelligence Culture in Uruguay

Writing from Montevideo, Jorge Jouroff examines the state of Uruguayan security and intelligence institutions and their relationship with that country's national culture. He cautions that any attempt to restructure the system needs to be wary of applying theoretical models that may not fit Uruguayan reality, even as he urges a careful evaluation of the resources available to carry out needed reforms. He suggests that, although the country does not enjoy a unique intelligence culture, it remains on the national agenda. Further, although he is aware that Uruguay will not likely have available to it the sophisticated technical resources of some other countries, he is confident that the analysis of intelligence can be a particular strength in Uruguay, and that this capability needs to be exploited. To start in that direction, he recommends that leaders identify the real reasons why the country should want an intelligence service, with an emphasis on its linkages with other tools of the state apparatus, rather than as an end in itself.

Recognizing that interagency cooperation in intelligence stems from a sustained consensus on common security challenges as seen by two or more countries, rather than by internal or external fiat, the author goes on to point out that, beyond such international agreements, each country has a right to define its own threats. Like other authors in this volume, Jouroff acknowledges the need for political backing across the society to put in place a viable, effective national intelligence system. This cannot be achieved immediately, but rather depends on the commitment of a succession of governments as part of overall national security policy.

Jouroff's own experience tells him that one of the pillars of a legitimate national intelligence system is having in place external oversight bodies such as the national congress. This in turn depends on having an appropriate national intelligence law. However, he does not call for the existence of a cadre of specialized civilians to be in change of the intelligence system itself, leaving us to infer that by this omission he accepts as a substitute the military and police bureaucracy already in place. Thus, in Uruguay, as in some other countries of the region, the concept of implanting civilian intelligence administrators in the intelligence services themselves, as a way to increase the efficacy of national intelligence, remains to be accomplished.

The Obligation of Bolivian Society to Construct a National Intelligence System

The influence that Bolivian military intelligence wields in support of the further development of the state is the theme addressed by Rear Admiral Raúl Mejía Ibáñez. In that light, it is important to remember that Bolivia, outside of the period of the Chaco War, has had no national intelligence system. Today, according to the author, the country does have some well-developed national intelligence sub-systems and some under development; however, they function in isolation from one another. What is missing is a central organization that could integrate the efforts of the existing entities. In his view, this situation represents an unacceptable danger for the state's highest-level decision makers, and is in fact a mistake.

Mejía Ibáñez finds that a national intelligence system is indispensable to national development as well as to national defense by allowing the state to safeguard both its security interests and its national objectives. He reminds readers that the absence of an intelligence system derailed the plans of President Gonzalo Sanchez de Lozada, who, as a result of depending only on the strategic intelligence advice of the Ministry of Government, reached incorrect conclusions with respect to the internal security situation. The result was that violence and chaos precipitated the fall of his administration and an interruption in the normal process of presidential succession.

In contrast, the author asserts that, even in the absence of a national intelligence system, the military intelligence service has made notable contributions by providing strategic assessments for national decision making. As an example, he describes the analytic capability of military intelligence in the government of General Hugo Banzer Suárez (1997-2001) during the social unrest that accompanied the so-called "Water War." Military intelligence suggested appropriate courses of action that were adopted and which resolved the problems.

To further establish the point, the author recounts that it was also military intelligence that later prepared analyses used by President Carlos Meza Gisbert. With these examples, Mejía Ibáñez declares in no uncertain terms that Bolivian military intelligence contributes not only to national defense, but also to the mitigation of internal crisis situations, working to preserve the unity and integrity of the state as well as of the government in power. To explain the efficacy of military intelligence, the author suggests that much credit is due the Army's Military Intelligence School, attended by members of all the military services as well as police officers and civilians, to include students from friendly countries.

The author does express some concern about the will of the political class to give positive consideration to the proposed National Security and Defense Act that is under review in the national Congress. This legislation would lay the groundwork for obtaining societal support for a national intelligence system. It would also begin to overcome the deficiency in the number of civilian professionals in the intelligence agencies and combat the stigma that still afflicts intelligence organizations as a result of earlier political activity, torture, and other human rights violations with which it is associated.

Taking a proactive stance, the author formulates a proposal to create a national intelligence system for Bolivia. It would establish an Intelligence Community under the military J-2, which already embraces the intelligence organizations of the three services, Army, Air Force, and Navy. It would broaden the J-2's jurisdiction to include the National Police and other national and regional entities. This arrangement would satisfy some important organizational ideals: it would be focused on national security as well as defense; it would serve the President directly as part of the National Defense Council; it would include both internal and external responsibilities, access to special funding, a Director appointed by the national Congress, and oversight by the Ministry of Finance and by a special Congressional Committee. Finally, the author suggests that additional elements of the national intelligence system would include the Ministry of Foreign Relations for foreign intelligence issues and the Ministry of Government for internal issues. To those would be added officials from the Migration Department as well as those from the elite Special Forces for narcotrafficking.

Understanding the Influence of National Culture on Ecuador's Intelligence System

Jaime Castillo of Ecuador explores Ecuadorian national culture and its influence on the makeup of the intelligence apparatus in that country. He begins by noting the contribution of civilian and military observers, as well as of military authorities themselves, who have written insightful essays about Ecuadorian intelligence activities. After 1979, intelligence at the national level achieved considerable institutionalization as a result of the National Security Law. It established a national intelligence entity called the National Intelligence Directorate within the General Secretariat of the National Security Council (COSENA). However, the author also notes that, as often happens in the area of security and defense, requisite attention to national intelligence has been eclipsed in the sense that any issue linked to it is resolved in the context of trying to improve civil-military relations. Thus, there remains a need for national legislation that reflects the singular importance of strategic intelligence in both national and international contexts.

The author considers that intelligence in Ecuador exists as a part of the armed forces, and because the society does not see it in any other light it is viewed as a threat to human rights and as a tool of governing authorities, rather than being a function of the State per se. Therefore, there is no concept that intelligence needs to be "reformed" to meet the society's needs. He nonetheless asserts that, in order for intelligence services to become the professional entities they need to be as an instrument for effective decision making by leaders across the nation, its organization and equipment should be under the control of civilian authorities.

In developing his ideas, Castillo establishes the value of "demilitarizing" the concept of intelligence, given that the range of intelligence activities suitable for a state go beyond the military realm to involve multidisciplinary analysis related to personal security, development, education, and international relations. In this regard, he hints at an argument he is likely reserving for another essay: that despite the 1998 Border Peace Treaty between Ecuador and Perú, which settled a decades-long conflict between the two countries, the Ecuadorian armed forces have retained their hegemony over national intelligence, leaving little room for the development of civilian specialists in strategic intelligence.

The author does make a revelation that calls into question the central authority of the National Intelligence Directorate: he confirms that the "Ecuadorian Public Forces" can undertake both internal and foreign intelligence activity without effective, centralized control. Rather, the NID simply serves a coordinating role.

The author agrees with other analysts of the region that the international exchange of information on transnational crime remains an obligation. An institutional example of such exchange exists in the "Bi-national Ecuador-Colombia Border Commission." The author recommends greater intelligence institutionalization in Ecuador to facilitate this type of information exchange because, otherwise, "those who feel threatened will seek other avenues to obtain it." He cites, and is supported by, the National Intelligence Strategy of the U.S. in this regard.

We should not lose sight of the idea that Castillo intends to alert us to the transcendent importance of strategic intelligence in all areas of national government. When this approach is adopted, taking full advantage of technology and knowledge, it will become a sound investment in good decision making.

Notable Evolution in Chilean National Intelligence

Chilean author Carolina Sancho Hirane confirms the impression held by many in Latin America: that this country has developed in the last decade—not without some hiccups—a consistent public policy concerning intelligence, characterized by the author as being "pre-active" in intent and "inclusive" in its formulation. She notes that three national organizations have managed this evolution: the Public Security Coordinating Council (1991-1993); the Public Security and Information Directorate (1993-2004); and since 2004, the National Intelligence Agency (ANI), which also heads up the National Intelligence System (SIE).

The author finds that the quality of intelligence produced in Chile is associated with the national political culture. In turn, this culture is reflected in the nature of the intelligence community: it abides by court decisions, respects the democratic nature of government and the constitutional rights of the people, and is guided by the principles of judicial authorization, proportionality, and care in the handling and use of information. The author gives us an inside look at the intelligence system through an examination of judicial oversight, showing that the complex, interconnected, and changeable threats and risks that populate the 21st century require a new perspective where thinking occurs not only in terms of alternative future scenarios, but also in terms of fresh, novel scenarios specifically tied to national objectives and interests.

Given those criteria, and despite undeniable progress in meeting them, the author argues for a more thorough modernization of public policy with respect to intelligence. She points out three areas for improvement: strategic intelligence, the public approach to intelligence, and the national intelligence community itself. She goes even further in suggesting that various public entities that can contribute in some way to strategic intelligence need to become part of the SIE, even though they have traditionally not been associated with intelligence. Notably, she has in mind the Foreign Ministry, whose absence she finds difficult to understand, given the country's needs and objectives.

In a similar vein, she finds it inexplicable that the Ministry of Energy is not a part of the SIE, given the role of energy in national development, and the fact that energy security has been threatened in recent years (the scarcity of which is abetted by supply restrictions from foreign sources). She argues for an intelligence perspective in the Energy Ministry to understand the complexity, diversity, and uniqueness of the relevant factors. The incorporation of such non-traditional government agencies into the National Intelligence System will determine the success or failure of its continuing evolution. The System needs timely, precise, and trustworthy information for the highest levels of state decision making to cut through information saturation with some efficiency.

Another Chilean author, Carlos Maldonado Prieto, offers fresh insight into the political influence on strategic intelligence in this country. He relates his conviction that, because intelligence is part of the defense policy of a country, the secret services have suffered a fate similar to that of the Chilean armed forces: the political elite has paid little attention to national security issues, and thus neither the armed forces nor intelligence have been assigned a clear mission.

This author also suggests that, because of this absence of leadership, national defense policy was mainly designed by the armed forces themselves. One result is that inadequate resources have been allocated to the defense sector, even though for several decades strategic intelligence has been considered a part of military intelligence. Thus, strategic intelligence has remained separated from the highest levels of decision making in the country. Of course, the author reminds us of the tragic period of the military dictatorship in Chile between 1973 and 1990, and of its significance for the development of national intelligence. During this period, intelligence services acted as political police dedicated to repressing and undermining opponents of the regime, thereby perpetrating grievous violations of human rights.

These unfortunate circumstances distorted the perception of the intelligence services among the political class, a fact reflected in public opinion. Military intelligence itself was accepted as a necessary evil. Indeed, several cases of political espionage did in fact take place between 1990 and 2005, perpetrated by Army and police intelligence operatives. Among the most notable episodes, with international repercussions, was the intelligence operation carried out in 2003 by military intelligence officials against the Argentine Consulate in Punta Arenas.

This affront to democratic government moved the Chilean governing coalition to carry out a gradual reform of the intelligence system, and to apply a strict legal framework. A civilian intelligence service was created with the intention of bringing reform to the military intelligence branches. In the end, the National Intelligence Agency was created to enforce respect for human rights as well as for legal and constitutional authorities. These developments came about after intense policy debates, sometimes laden with continuing prejudices against intelligence. The ANI was placed in charge of three areas: terrorism, organized crime, and counterintelligence. Other areas, such as economic intelligence, industrial espionage, and the proliferation of weapons of mass destruction, remained unassigned by the enacting legislation. Additionally, ANI may not conduct intelligence operations, nor can it penetrate banking secrecy.

Nonetheless, the weight of ongoing events has meant that ANI continues to gain the flexibility to address a much greater range of issues than formally established by law. Such is the case with economic and energy intelligence, as well as freedom to investigate neo-Nazi groups. Despite this progress, the author recognizes the continuing need for ANI to develop public confidence through its respect for legal constraints. Like Sancho Hirane, this author recommends that other governmental institutions become a part of ANI. Those should include the Chancellery, Customs, the Gendarmería, and the government's financial analytic unit. Additionally, when a National Intelligence School is established, it should be dedicated to the joint education of intelligence analysts from civilian, military, and police organizations.

The Way Ahead for Guatemala's Intelligence Culture

The combined work of Grisel M. Capó and Werner F. Ovalle rests on their examination of the multicultural Guatemalan scene. Their own experience and observations are supplemented by their survey of in-country security, defense, and intelligence experts. They find that, despite reforms undertaken following the extended period of armed conflict in the country, Guatemala is only now beginning to implant a legal framework to overcome the effects of volatile security and intelligence institutions. There remains a tendency to favor police intelligence over national, strategic intelligence.

The authors lament, like others in this book, that the chief intelligence agency in the country, the Strategic Analysis Secretariat, has seen eight directors come and go in the past eight years. This situation signals the lack of effective national policy. However, the authors do express approval of changes in the other main intelligence institution in the country—the General Civilian Intelligence Directorate—which, following the Chilean police intelligence model, has since 2005 had some success against organized crime and serious problems of delinquency.

These authors uncover another vulnerability of Guatemalan national intelligence, again similar to what has been observed in other countries of the region: that the military establishment maintains its hegemony in national intelligence through the Military Intelligence Directorate. It is difficult for civilian intelligence professionals to gain a foothold because of the usual wholesale replacement of civilian intelligence officials with each change of government. | 53

Furthermore, neither the population at large nor national political leaders act in accord with a culture of prevention in the face of vulnerabilities, risks, and threats, an approach which perpetuates a culture of social violence. Even as ignorance and negativity about the intelligence function abound in the country, some individuals and groups are seeking to overcome this problem by finding ways to improve civil-military relations. One avenue is through civil society forums such as the "Defense Community" and the "Guatemalan Network for Democratic Security." The authors are convinced that the lack of an appropriate intelligence culture among national leaders has undermined the existing institutions, permitting private intelligence groups to flourish.

The authors maintain that a culture of prevention can be implanted in multi-ethnic, multicultural and multilingual Guatemala as part of a full implementation of national peace accords. With the newly promulgated National Intelligence Law in place, they also see as necessary the recruitment and training of specialists in strategic intelligence as a way to enhance civil-military relations.

National Intelligence in Costa Rica and Its Deficiencies

Paul Chaves describes the historical evolution of the national intelligence service in his country, by name the Intelligence and Security Directorate (DIS). He recounts the several failed attempts to bring about a more effective, professional service. As it stands, the DIS has a police orientation, and is furthermore linked to successive governments rather than to the state, which works against its professionalism. Specifically, the author finds fault with the ultimate consumers of intelligence, namely the President and the Office of the President, who tend not to have a sound understanding of the intelligence function. His criticism on that score extends to many of the successive Directors of the DIS.

Further developing this line of thought, the author suggests that Costa Rican national security and its democratic institutions have thus far not suffered appreciably from the absence of an effective national intelligence agency. This is so for the same reason that the country has managed to get along without an army: It lacks a sense of being threatened by other countries. In fact, the only threat seen to Costa Rican stability is that stemming from narcotrafficking and associated crimes. To confront that threat, several security institutions, none of them associated with the DIS, do operate with an acceptable level of proficiency and professionalism.

The author sees considerable danger in not having a national intelligence agency that is capable of carrying out appropriate operations under legal and societal oversight. This situation results from negligence on the part of both the civil society (the "political class") and government leaders. These groups would ultimately be responsible if a new threat to national security and democratic stability were to arise without being foreseen and addressed by the DIS. In addition, we can observe that this security vulnerability has serious ramifications in reducing the potential for regional cooperation against transnational threats, to include terrorism, narcotrafficking, trafficking in arms and people, and international organized crime.

The Construction of an Intelligence Culture in Spain

Fernando Velasco, Rubén Arcos, and Diego Navarro together explain that in Spain a new impetus toward an intelligence culture has come from a growing relationship between universities and the intelligence services, originally stimulated by a democratic impulse flowing from the Constitution of 1978. The new Constitution gave a boost to civil culture, which has combined with a "political socialization" of the intelligence services. The most notable outcome thus far has been the creation of the National Intelligence Center (CNI), which has replaced the Defense Information Headquarters (CESID), as a result of a 2002 law. This law embodied the aspirations of Spanish society; namely, to have an effective, focused and modern intelligence service that can address national and international issues, but that is also clearly subject to legal and constitutional oversight.

The authors contend that an essential precursor to a national intelligence culture stems from the society's understanding of why intelligence services are needed. That is, the intelligence services not only provide for the security and defense of the country, but also are central to the protection and advancement of the rights and interests of the entire population. The authors do, however, recognize that to achieve this ideal, Spanish society must set aside long-standing prejudices and distortions about intelligence that were formed in the pre-democratic era.

The authors review the CNI's attempts to foment a positive intelligence culture, as it has tried to acquaint the population at large with the real nature of strategic, national intelligence. They conclude that the effort is well underway, and point to the intelligence curriculum in their own universities (University of King Juan Carlos and University of Charles III of Madrid) as evidence of the assertion. They also contend that the publication of the first academic intelligence journal in Spain is an integral part of the process.

The authors go on to spell out four strategies that their universities are undertaking to further develop a positive intelligence culture in the country: engaging practitioners and institutions to build on accumulated experience; employing openness and dialogue to foster an understanding of topics related to national intelligence; promoting an exchange of ideas; and bringing transparency through various communications media, including the promotion of books, articles, and other publications that bring further clarity to national intelligence.

Additionally, the authors allude to the importance of research, including doctoral dissertations, to build ties with universities and research centers in other countries where an intelligence culture is already well established. In this effort they are supported by the consensus that now obtains in Spain between the society at large and the country's intelligence community.

Nature and Characteristics of the Cuban Intelligence Services

Beginning with an historical perspective, Cuban author and former intelligence agent Juan Manuel Reyes-Alonso takes us back to 1959 to review the origins of the government's intelligence services. At that time, the clandestine, revolutionary anti-Batista movement created the Investigative Service of the Rebel Army (DIER), putting it in charge of police functions as well as of intelligence and counterintelligence. According to the author's sources, in 1960, as Fidel Castro seized power across the island, he made two new intelligence services, the State Security Agency (DSE) and the General Intelligence Directorate (DGI), subordinate to the Interior Ministry (MININT).

The DSE was designated to operate within Cuba, and assumed the counterintelligence role previously assigned to the DIER. At the same time, the DGI focused on foreign intelligence and counterintelligence. The author emphasizes that the DGI was headed by the fearsome Comandante Manuel Piñeiro Losada (pseudonym *Barbarroja* and cryptonym M-1). In contrast with the DSE, which did not have Soviet advisors, the DGI did depend heavily on those advisors, especially after 1965. Meanwhile, the Revolutionary Armed Forces (FAR) built its own secret services: the Military Intelligence Directorate (DIM) and the Military Counterintelligence Directorate (CIM), both of which maintained interaction with the DGI.

As this information shows, the author is very explicit in his description, and he makes it clear from the start that the Cuban intelligence services played a key role in the Castro regime. He notes that officials of the DIER, and then of the DSE, were well-educated, many of them having studied and lived in the U.S. before the start of the regime. This meant that intelligence and counterintelligence officials could infiltrate communities of Cubans and Americans in the U.S., and gain a valuable perspective on the U.S. government and its own intelligence services. Without doubt, this operational potential was greatly reinforced by the systematic training and technical and economic support of the Soviet KGB and other intelligence services of the Socialist Bloc, such as those of East Germany and Bulgaria.

Reyes-Alonso points out that, in contrast with the KGB, the Cuban DGI emphasizes the recruitment of agents based on ideological affinity, rather than through cash incentives, as a way to overcome the DGI's economic and logistical deficiencies. In short, its HUMINT effort is highly effective. The dedication of Cuban HUMINT experts is essential to that success, given the lack of a positive, socialist model for them to emulate. Among the interesting details confirmed by the author: the principal divisions of Cuban intelligence are Department M-I, focused on the U.S.; M-II, focused on Latin America; and M-III, charged with strategic intelligence *analysis*.

For the author, Department M-V is not only the most secretive and compartmented division of the DGI, but it is distinctive for its autonomy. Its finances remain a secret, even to the DGI's comptroller. Only a very restricted group in the DGI and from the highest levels of the Castro regime know the true financial resources and real identities of the covert M-V operators. The author indicates that these covert agents are very well-prepared and can insinuate themselves undetected in the country to which they have been assigned, even to the point of becoming citizens of the target country.

The next Department, M-VI, exists expressly to engage in corporate espionage and to get around the U.S. economic embargo of Cuba.

Reyes-Alonso places a spotlight on a 1989 episode in Cuba that has been widely ignored: the secrets behind the "1st and 2nd Causes." These were judicial processes against Cuban officials who were found to be associated with narcotrafficking and with other corruption. He alleges that many of these government officials were operating on behalf of the government, and even of Fidel himself. What was especially damaging to Cuban intelligence services from this episode was the witch hunt that Raúl Castro instituted to remove those officials who, in his view, did not serve his purposes in the power games he was playing.

Finally, like many critics of the Castro regime,[94] the author is convinced that the intelligence services have played a fundamental and powerful role in keeping the Castro regime in power. Fidel survived the regimes of 10 U.S. Presidents and some 630 assassination plots against him. The intelligence and security services have made it possible for the only communist government of the hemisphere to survive, with the consequence that it can continue to undermine democratic rule in the entire region, now with the support of additional resources that accompany the tight relationship which the Cuban government is maintaining with Hugo Chavez's administration.

Perspectives on U.S. Intelligence Culture

Jon Wiant offers his views on U.S. intelligence culture, and identifies a significant duality in the way it is seen by the country's citizens: whereas on

---

94 See the interview article, "Cuba ya vive la era post-Fidel Castro: Brian Latell," in the Mexico City daily *El Universal*, 22 January 2007, where Brian Latell, who for more than 30 years worked as a Latin America analyst with the CIA, and for 15 years was a member of the National Intelligence Council, asserts the following about Cuban intelligence: "It is one of the five best intelligence services, in my opinion. I consider that along with that of the U.S., Great Britain, Russia and Israel, Cuba's is among the very best."

the one hand, national intelligence needs to be reinvigorated in the wake of the 9/11 attacks to neutralize the continuing threat, there exists at the same time a notable reluctance to see additional intelligence vigor because it can threaten Constitutional protections. Despite this ambivalence, the author finds that the issue of how to apply intelligence to safeguard the internal security of the U.S. has contributed to fruitful discussion and action.

In further exploring this duality, Wiant concludes that there is always a variable, interpretive aspect in the application of the diverse laws that govern intelligence activities, whereby their interpretation does not depend on the court system but rather on Congress itself. It is Congress that determines whether an intelligence law has been violated. With that in mind, the author points out the controversial interpretation of the Foreign Intelligence Surveillance Act (FISA), which requires a judicial order to tap the communications of an individual in the U.S. who is suspected of having contact with foreign agents—potential enemies of the U.S. and its policies.

For Wiant, this problem comes to a head when the degree of intelligence vigilance brings about a technical violation of law, rather than a violation of its intent, simply because the legislation in question did not foresee the dramatic changes in the means of personal communication, which in effect make the law irrelevant. The author voices his worry that the relevance of the law is debated only in Congress, a place teeming with political partisanship, rather than in the court system. Other than in this discontinuity between law and reality in the U.S., the author considers that few real, cultural differences exist in the approach to intelligence activities taken by the English-speaking and non-English-speaking countries of the hemisphere.

Referring back to his personal experiences in the intelligence profession, the author (who was involved in the investigation of the Iran-Contra case), remains convinced of the obligation of intelligence agencies, as well as of individual practitioners, to protect sources and methods. If they do not, they would expose themselves and the intelligence system to even greater danger and greater scrutiny by Congress. Wiant draws attention to the honesty and loyalty to the country and to the profession that prevails among U.S. intelligence professionals. An examplar of these virtues was Nathan Hale, whose statue is found in front of CIA headquarters, and who famously declared, "I regret that I have but one life to give for my country." Wiant then relates an interesting story about former CIA Director Bill Casey, who expressed a somewhat different view of Hale's intelligence professionalism.

On another plane, the author asserts that, despite the importance attached to individual initiative in the U.S., over the past 20 years, the belief has grown that a team approach to intelligence activities is required to attain successful results. This philosophy is not unfavorable to the application of imagination, innovation, and a willingness to take risks. However, in this context, the author expresses concern about the difficulty of reaching a satisfactory balance between individual initiative and individual responsibility.

Wiant goes on to explore other vulnerabilities of U.S. intelligence, particularly in the area of human-source intelligence (HUMINT). He argues that a characteristic bureaucratic formalism as well as a "frightful impatience" in U.S. intelligence circles mean that careful and productive HUMINT activity cannot flourish. One is reminded of the Chinese proverb "Make of patience an art and of hope a virtue."

Of interest is the author's claim that the principal collectors of intelligence for the U.S. government, in the cultural, economic, social, and political realm, that is, information useful for policy development, comes not from the CIA but rather from the Foreign Service of the Department of State. Information from this Service, in the view of the author, makes up 60 or 70 percent of the President's Daily Brief. Despite this reality, the author notes that in recent years the intelligence role of the Foreign Service has been undermined for various reasons, seriously affecting U.S. intelligence capabilities. In light of this observation, he thinks that national-level intelligence leaders need to give greater priority to resourcing this Service, rather than other Community agencies, to give a pragmatic boost to HUMINT.

In any event, Wiant is aware of the need to continue gathering information about the intentions and policies of foreign powers through a clandestine service. He does observe that the existing CIA-based Clandestine Service would find a strong complement in the Foreign Service. Such collaboration with the Foreign Service would allow formidable interoperability, possibly overcoming some of the fragmentation that now characterizes the Intelligence Community. Finally, he notes that it might also be possible to take a long-term approach to HUMINT programs if the planning horizon were lengthened to resemble that of the more technical U.S. intelligence programs such as those involving satellite collection.

Another revealing perspective comes from Bowman H. Miller, who shows that tradition, history, myths, legends, stories, anecdotes, language, and shared national image have all played a strong formative role in U.S. national intelligence. Looking back through history, he finds that from Revolutionary times—from 1776—many of its citizens have seen their country in heroic terms, imputing to it a divine obligation to lead the world and serve it as a permanent guarantor of basic values such as liberty, peace, justice, and equality of opportunity. America, in the view of this author, has thus seen itself as a "city on the hill," and this attitude has justified U.S. intervention in other countries in promotion of universal values, namely expanding the reach of liberty and democracy. Still, the author reminds us that there is not in this country a single point of view with respect to strategic thinking, as there does not exist a unitary national culture.

The author goes on to show that, despite some known successes, U.S. national intelligence has for decades suffered from errors and poor judgment with respect to just how the country might most fruitfully interact with other countries. In the first several years of the 21st century, the U.S. has suffered from two national intelligence failures: first, a failure by omission, in not anticipating the attacks of 9/11, and second, by commission, in presuming that Saddam Hussein possessed weapons of mass destruction. As a result of these developments, the Intelligence Community was expected to improve, and found itself under greater congressional oversight. The author finds fault with an overemphasis on security threats by defense officials, and with the lingering focus on the events of 9/11.

Continuing his review of the national intelligence landscape in his country, the author points out an additional factor: the proliferation of pundits and of sources of information. Specifically, he considers that, despite warnings against the U.S. invasion of Iraq made by the U.S. Intelligence Community, and especially by State Department analysts, the press and mass communication outlets all failed to carry out their traditional, independent, and objective investigative mission by not reporting critically on the plans, policies, and intentions of the U.S. with respect to Iraq in 2002 and 2003. At the same time, Miller points out that, despite the Community's intention to remain secretive, the fact that two to three million people in government have access to intelligence information, and live in a liberal and open society, in practice means that leaks of sensitive information are rather common.

In another area, Miller confirms that, in the U.S., personal privacy continues to be a right protected by laws, which also accord an individual access to government information about the individual. This right has been tested by the USA PATRIOT Act, which has fostered "warrantless wiretapping." Thus, the author finds that, although there is not a unitary culture in the country despite the call for greater unity of effort expressed by the National Intelligence Strategy, some cultural proclivities remain very clear with respect to intelligence. Miller also notes that U.S. counterterrorism experts find that in the past 40 years the defense and intelligence apparatus has not kept pace with the highly mobile and secretive networks of fourth-generation (asymmetric) warfare. He notes that intelligence leaders do understand that such conflict will be long-lasting and not susceptible to being won with high explosives. Rather, the new warfare is fundamentally a war of ideas.

Miller suggests that the national intelligence culture of the U.S. reflects several facets of its overall culture as well as its strategic culture. That is, even as there is a focus on threats, the overriding aim is to place the country in position to handle the tide of globalization by ensuring global coverage fitting for a global superpower. All this even as the Intelligence Community concentrates its resources on the most urgent issues. This well-placed author remains convinced that U.S. political authorities will continue to demand that they not be surprised by facts, threats, or other phenomena that may affect the country, even as it is understood that this mission is supremely difficult to accomplish.

About the Author

Jorge Serrano Torres, a Peruvian, holds degrees in Public Administration, Law, and Communications. He specialized in Strategic Intelligence and Counterintelligence at the Peruvian National Intelligence School, and studied at the Peruvian Diplomatic School. He is an active member of Strategos, a Peruvian institute for intelligence analysis and dissemination, and offers courses at the Army Intelligence School. He is also a faculty member at Ricardo Palma University, where he holds the Mariátegui Chair and teaches courses in intelligence and regional, international relations. Serrano also lectures at the Peruvian National University in San Marcos, and is a consultant with the Research Center for the Development of Justice, which fights corruption and promotes personal security within the framework of Peruvian and regional justice systems. He has also served as advisor to the German Agency for International Cooperation and Development in its Good Government Program. He additionally contributes regularly to the multilingual "Voltaire" network, with headquarters in France and links to the International Press Agency. His essays have been published in ten countries. He may be contacted at *jas_606@hotmail.com and antonio3032003@yahoo.es.*

REFLECTIONS ON INTELLIGENCE CULTURE: CAREER ENGAGEMENTS OF A U.S. CIVIL AND MILITARY INTELLIGENCE OFFICER

Jon Wiant, with Russell G. Swenson

> *Habitually, Americans associate secrecy with privilege and sinister maneuvering, both of which go against their grain. As a result, the paper trail documenting secret intelligence activities surfaces only in bits and pieces combed from such unconventional sources as narrowly circulated memoirs and quietly commissioned reports stored in archives.*[95]

Why is intelligence today such a salient feature of U.S. foreign affairs and national security? Historically it had its importance during times of conflict, but generally was not an activity that enjoyed public esteem or much financial support. That changed with World War II, when for the first time we mobilized the intellectual resources of the country to engage in intelligence work for national security. Intelligence mobilization has remained a feature of U.S. culture since that time.

At the same time, the notion of national intelligence in popular culture, in the chords of memory that bind the citizens of this country, has been transformed strictly from its association with secrecy—and its equation with espionage—to a point, from about 1975, where there reigns a two-sided, schizophrenic view of intelligence in American society. On the one hand, we have the view that national intelligence must be continually enhanced, that it must be made more extensive, that it must be made ever more pervasive, in order to meet threats such as that from terrorism—which is difficult to define, but manifest in the events of 11 September 2001. The other side of the coin is wariness about this enterprise, whereby it is seen as the very enemy of the Constitution

---

95 Edward F. Sayle, "The Historical Underpinnings of the U.S. Intelligence Community," *International Journal of Intelligence and Counterintelligence* 1, no. 1 (Spring 1986), 1. In this light, the Association for Diplomatic Studies and Training Foreign Affairs Oral History Project (*http://www.adst.org/index.html*) has recently interviewed Jon Wiant about his intelligence career.

that it was created to support. My own career played out squarely within this tension, between the clear purpose of intelligence in supporting national security, and the question of how much we should engage in this business at home to make ourselves more secure.

U.S. Intelligence Culture in the Hemispheric Context

In Latin America, national intelligence, including the military intelligence apparatus, has been employed to suppress internal opposition. Further, detailed Constitutions characteristic of many countries in the region can take on the flavor of regulations rather than general guiding principles. In the U.S. case, the Constitution, with its relatively few amendments, remains largely a repository of general principles, including the first ten amendments, known as the Bill of Rights. Thus, in the U.S. it may be easier for us to fall back on those general guiding principles than it is for intelligence professionals in the non-English speaking parts of the Hemisphere, who in intending philosophically to support their Constitution rather than a particular political administration, may be poorly served. That is, in some countries, the Constitution will likely reflect a particular administration's view of what is permitted by government agents and, even if not, it is not unknown for a Constitution to be observed in the breach, leaving an intelligence operative without an ethical safety net.[96]

Nonetheless, while we do have a deep sense of constitutionalism in the U.S., the sense of it may be deeper than the reality. That is to say, our attachment to the Bill of Rights has great symbolic appeal, and yet, on any particular day, we will find significant voices in this country that advocate positions that seem to be fundamentally inconsistent with the Bill of Rights. But with that having been said, we collectively share this ideal, and every intelligence officer is brought into service with the basic catechism that says we may be breaking the laws abroad, but it is critical to us that we be fundamentally attentive to our own domestic laws.

An essential truth to be understood about national intelligence practices in the U.S. is that our intelligence-related laws are not perceived to be the same as everyday laws. To make that point more clear: Many years ago, during the covert action program in Central America, particularly in Nicaragua, we had an amendment, the Boland Amendment, that imposed significant restrictions on what activities we could conduct, and attached to that was the idea that

---

96 *Semana.com* (Colombia), "Dos Bolivias: La aprobación de la nueva Carta Magna hizo que el país se polarizara más allá de lo previsible. Muchos temen guerra civil, la partición del país, o las dos." 1 December 2007, URL: *http://www.semana.com/wf_InfoArticulo.aspx?IdArt=108049.*

we could not spend money on certain kinds of operations.[97] The prohibitions themselves were fundamentally consistent with our stated policy. The problem was that there was a growing gap between the stated policy and the actual policy we were pursuing in Central America. At one point I was spun up about this concern, and I went to a very senior official in my organization, telling him that I had been looking very closely at this activity and it appeared that we are in violation of the law. And the senior official said, "Jon, this law is different from, for example, bank robbing laws. There, it's pretty cut and dried. But in these kinds of laws, you are not against the law, until a majority of Congress says you are against the law, and we don't have a majority saying that right now."

There is an interpretive aspect to the enforcement of a range of laws that are central to how we conduct the intelligence business. The interpretation depends not so much on the court system, where we think justice is delivered, but rather on the actions of the legislative branch. That branch determines whether a law has been violated. Similarly, today we face concerns about the interpretation of the Foreign Intelligence Surveillance Act (FISA), which requires a legal warrant prior to "wiretapping" individuals within the U.S. who are in communication with foreign or non-governmental opponents of the U.S. and its policies.[98] So-called "warrantless wiretaps" by definition occur in violation of this law, because it stipulates that any domestic electronic surveillance will be conducted within the framework of this statute. Although such intelligence targeting is against the law in the technical sense of being against the FISA, some people do argue that the problem is that the language of the statute did not anticipate the structure of contemporary communications. And so, because the structure of the communications systems is so changed, that law is irrelevant. And if we wish to say a law is irrelevant, we have the courts to say that. But the debate occurs in a Congress where political partisanship reigns, and not so far at the highest level of the court system.

Thus, this aspect of cultural difference between the English-speaking and non-English speaking parts of the hemisphere is not so great as anticipated. And this is for many an uncomfortable observation to make. Another example comes from E. Howard Hunt's recent book.[99] He did not have a great reputation at CIA; his career accomplishments were modest. But at the White House,

---

97 See GAO *Red Book* report B-201260, 11 September 1984, for a legal opinion by the U.S. General Accounting (now Government Accountability) Office. This opinion outlines the prohibitions identified by the Boland Amendment. URL: *http://redbook.gao.gov/14/fl0067296.php*.

98 For the text of the Foreign Intelligence Surveillance Act, see *http://www.access.gpo.gov/uscode/title50/chapter36_.html*. In 2007, a "modernization" of the FISA was enacted, labeled the "Protect America Act of 2007." See *http://www.whitehouse.gov/news/releases/2007/08/20070806-5.html*.

99 E. Howard Hunt, *An American Spy: My Secret History in the CIA* (New York: Wiley, 2007).

his job was to forge or alter historical cables from the Kennedy Administration to establish that that earlier President was the central figure in the decision to overthrow Vietnam's Ngo Dinh Diem in 1963, as well as being involved in the Vietnamese leader's subsequent death. The purpose of Hunt's work was to provide a controlled leak of the cables to discredit Kennedy, and by extension to discredit Ted Kennedy in his potential Presidential campaign. This Executive wrongdoing, involving the Chief of Staff to the President, was a matter of everyday business. And nowhere in Hunt's account does anyone consider this approach wrong, or that "this is against the law." Those involved did wonder what to do if they were caught, which is a rather different question. As we ponder intelligence operatives involved in this way in the White House, we can look back and say, "That was a pretty scary period."

When Congress decides to hold hearings to bring to the attention of the public the dimensions of such **alleged** illegality—we had similar hearings about Iran-Contra—we have the secret parts of intelligence under the spotlight of a public inquiry. In these cases, issues are raised that get too scary for people to want to go further—questions that we simply do not want to ask because we are afraid of the answer that might follow. Unfortunately, the examination of this dilemma has largely been left to the movies where "Enemy of the State" has taken on a multitude of meanings, many of which are indicative of this public fear.

I look at this situation as someone who had almost an entire year of his life consumed by the Iran-Contra inquiry. I once calculated how many hours I spent being deposed and I'm not anything but a bit player in terms of long-term involvement in the program, but I was a witness to everything. It's very uncomfortable if you are caught in this central dilemma of intelligence, which in fact is reinforced in the Central Intelligence Act of 1949—that it is our statutory obligation to protect sources and methods.[100] At the same time, there is a Constitutional obligation to reveal the very things that we are sworn to protect, if that revelation is central to uncovering or explicating a potential wrongdoing. There is a kind of irony that the man whose name holds the greatest stature in the CIA, Richard Helms, perjured himself in front of Congress by not revealing sources and methods.[101] We all look back on him as the exemplar of all that an

---

[100] According to CIA spokesman Edmund Cohen, in "Cold War Documentation, National Security, and the Fullest Possible Accounting: Restriction vs. Access," at the 25 September 1998 Cold War Conference on the Power of Free Inquiry and Cold War International History, "The Director of Central Intelligence's responsibility and authority to protect intelligence sources and methods is found in the National Security Act of 1947 and the CIA Act of 1949, as amended, as well as in Executive Order 12958." *https://www.cia.gov/news-information/speeches-testimony/1998/cohen_speech_092598.html.*

[101] Thomas Powers, *The Man Who Kept the Secrets: Richard Helms and the CIA* (New York: Knopf, 1979).

intelligence officer should be. When he was given the questions, he determined that the more important thing was his fidelity to the cardinal principles of the intelligence business rather than to answer the questions of elected Congressional representatives. To betray the name of a source who has provided things to us—even with the understanding that we will do things to ensure the source's safety—jeopardizes the fundamental circumstances under which we operate, and reflects the **potential** jeopardy of detailed Congressional oversight. On the other hand, we cannot have institutions that have values that are inconsistent and that are fundamentally in conflict with the society which created them and which they support. In 1775 our political ancestors with the Continental Congress established a Committee of Secret Correspondence to fund secretly some agents in England and France. One year later this same Committee expressed reluctance to report to the newly independent Congress for fear of jeopardizing sources and methods.[102] The issue has been with us a long time and continues to run like a *leit motiv* through the operational oversight relationship.

Cultural Values Embodied by U.S. Intelligence Officers

What is the appeal of the secret life? What is the appeal of a life where every morning you cross a perimeter, a boundary, a barrier, that separates you from society? You go to the workplace, show your badge, and enter your pass code, and it is not just a practical security measure, but a philosophical one in a big sense. In doing this we establish ourselves as part of a secret order. It has a kind of Freemasonry quality to it. And since it is not transparent, the public's notion of our business is in fact made more exciting by its exclusiveness and by its very opaqueness. And it is rendered to the public largely through fiction.[103]

While I was initially trained at Fort Holabird in 1965 as a counterintelligence special agent, I started my operational work in intelligence after being cross-trained as a case officer—as a kind of paramilitary case officer. When I was in case officer training, I learned to spot, assess, develop, and recruit a mid-level official in some Eastern European defense ministry. In fact, my first operational assignment as a case officer was in Vietnam, when none of the training seemed to have any relevance to my source, which was somebody who could get into the secret jungle zone. So instead of looking for a mid-level official, I got a person who is a rattan-maker, charcoal-maker, who could get impressed into

---

102 Center for the Study of Intelligence, *Intelligence in the War of Independence*, Intelligence Techniques: Secrecy and Protection, posted 15 March 2007 at *https://www.cia.gov/library/center-for-the-study-of-intelligence/csi-publications/books-and-monographs/intelligence/intelltech.html*.

103 Wesley Britton, *Beyond Bond: Spies in Fiction and Film* (New York: Greenwood Press, 2005).

The author as a young soldier in Vietnam.
Source: Author.

a porter column out in the jungle and taken to where there were secrets. This was a whole different kind of agent, and it has a kind of romance to it because the whole concept of identity is in play and because behind this wall that separates us from others and from our family, we have this secret self that is kind of appealing. I always thought that one of the differences in the personal relationship versus the institutional relationship is that we are committed to a greater fidelity in that institutional relationship—the relationship with an intelligence organization—than in the most sacred personal relationship, which is the trust of a marriage. Notably, one is compelled to be far more revelatory about the inner self in the relationship with an intelligence institution than ever seems to be the case in a marriage.

Patriotism is expressed in our intelligence duty and is nurtured in our mythology. We have for example the statue of Nathan Hale at the front of CIA. This spy who is about to be hung says, supposedly, that "I regret that I have but one life to give for my country." Director of Central Intelligence William Casey wanted that statue removed. "Why should we have a statue to a man who failed on his first mission, and then did not say that his regret was that he had failed on his intelligence mission?"[104] In my own moments of self-reflection I too regret that I can experience but one career in intelligence. This has been just a wonderful place for me to work—where else could I have done these exciting things—things that I would like to do again? And it's incidental that it's public service.

---

104 CIA Home Page story, "A Look Back—the Story of Nathan Hale," at *https://www.cia.gov/news-information/featured-story-archive/nathan-hale.html*, posted 20 September 2007. Also see "Nathan Hale" in Masters of the Intelligence Art series at *http://huachuca-www.army.mil/History/PDFS/MHALE.PDF*.

Recently I received the National Intelligence Distinguished Service Medal, the highest medal that comes from the Community, and as I listened to the recitation of my diverse activities, I'm thinking, "My God, that was fun!"

Intelligence as a Military or Paramilitary Function

If you are working in intelligence, there is absolutely no substitute for military service prior to going into the intelligence business. Service in the military or in combat support gives you some intimacy with the needs of an operational consumer. I have long thought that my success in the early part of my intelligence career was inextricably related to my success as a young artillery soldier. I had come to know military subjects pretty well, and when I became a military intelligence official I had some understanding of the relationship between the use of information and subsequent outcomes.

Recently, I have been working on an "anthropology in intelligence" study to see if we can develop a better understanding of the distinct operational and analytical cultures that are present in the 16 agencies that make up the Intelligence Community. My conceptualization of culture is very much influenced by work I did while a graduate student at Cornell, focusing on Burma. I had been impressed by the ways in which function affected the structure of social groups and how the demands of the larger environment in which the social group existed sharply influenced both power and authority in the organization. As I examined the contemporary Intelligence Community, one of the things that stood out to me as a defining attribute of different intelligence institutions was the steepness of the decision hierarchy. We can consider that such a hierarchy is more or less another form of asymmetric conflict—conflict between superiors and subordinates. In military intelligence one negative outcome of this steep hierarchy has been the opportunity afforded high-level intelligence officials to disregard competing intelligence estimates. It was a dark day for intelligence in 1967 when intelligence estimates of enemy numbers in Vietnam were disregarded in this way.[105] When there is a hotly contested intelligence issue, and the boss of an organization determines such limitations to analysis, then the organization can never really be good. Likewise, today if you are told that you cannot use the term "insurgent" for policy reasons, then it is very hard to come up with language that describes the factions that, for example, are in conflict in Iraq.

A central cultural question regarding U.S. intelligence is "What is its function? Is its function primarily military, regardless of whether a uni-

|69

---

105 Harold P. Ford, *CIA and the Vietnam Policymakers: Three Episodes 1962-1968* (Washington, DC: Center for the Study of Intelligence, 1998), 140.

formed service or civilians are involved? If we go back to the legislation in 1947, and the creation of the CIA, the purpose is laid out clearly to avoid experiencing another Pearl Harbor-style attack. The primary function of intelligence, national intelligence, strategic intelligence, therefore, is avoiding strategic surprise. But I have quibbled with that interpretation all along, because intelligence does many things.

The idea of all intelligence somehow being related to the military or to a military sense of national security has been very problematic for the transition of our organizations. Maintaining a long intelligence relationship with Vietnam, or interpreting the issue of changing relationships with China, involves things that are far broader, and that are far more varied, than the issue of strategic warning of military capabilities. At the end of the Cold War period, as we learned with the devaluation of the Mexican peso, an economic or banking decision can have profound strategic implications for our national well-being in realms far afield from estimating military-related intentions and capabilities.

Intelligence, Surveillance, and U.S. Domestic Security

The question of how intelligence may be used for internal security in the U.S. is the most important issues now facing our society. The outcome of that debate strongly affects how we envision our defining cultural institutions. Having been deeply involved in issues of the 1960s that provoked the call for reform in this area has caused me to consider how we got to that point. My understanding of how we became involved in surveillance for homeland security during the Vietnam War is both less sinister than many have made it, and more worrisome for that fact. The programs evolved not out of a determination to set the Constitution aside, but rather had their origins in things that would make sense to anyone, and that I would argue were legal. But the programs grew to be too robust, for lack of attentiveness or of oversight.

The 1949 Delimitations Agreement set out the spheres of responsibility among the FBI and the counterintelligence arms of the military services—who would have the lead in responsibility for subversion, espionage investigations, sabotage, and the like in the United States.[106] The agreement established that for matters within the jurisdiction of a military base, the lead investigative responsibility is that of the counterintelligence organization of the uniformed service. It was meant to keep intelligence "spooks" from bumping into each other, and it grew out of the concern for communist infiltration of American institutions in the early years of the Cold War period. Thus, if the incident were to take place at

---

106 See National Counterintelligence Center, *Counterintelligence in World War II*, Ed. Frank J. Rafalko, Vol 2, Chapter 1, n.d. *http://www.fas.org/irp/ops/ci/docs/ci2/2ch1_e.htm#fbimi.*

Fort Carson, an Army base, then the Army CI people would take the lead and go first. That concept is important for understanding how the surveillance of antiwar demonstrations came about.

The first action that transcended protest, moving into illegality, happened in 1965, with the sabotage of the rail line going into the Oakland, California, Army Terminal. Army counterintelligence therefore had the initial responsibility to surveil antiwar protestors, whether at Berkeley or at Stanford or at San Francisco City College. Later in 1965, U.S. troops were sent into Watts in South Los Angeles to put down serious riots and racial violence. This was transformational in the sense that the protests had escalated from the confrontational but relatively nonviolent civil rights movement in the Southeastern U.S. to what may be characterized as insurgent actions. The level of violence was sufficient that the president of the U.S. decided to commit troops for the first time since 1943 to put down a domestic disturbance.[107] From an intelligence perspective, the interesting thing was that, when the airborne troops were brought in, the commander asked for an intelligence briefing on the hostile forces. He asked the police department—paraphrasing—"Don't we have a military intelligence unit here?" The immediate answer: "Yes, we have nationwide military intelligence by region, and then field offices in large cities, for the purpose of doing background investigations, physical security, and occasionally espionage cases." The local commander from the Los Angeles field office admitted, "We don't have a clue." So the airborne commander says, "We have U.S. military forces committed here, and you're telling me that you don't have a clue? You are relieved of duty!"

After that, things turned around pretty quickly. Now we had two internal threats that we began to work on from within the military intelligence structure. One was the threat from the antiwar movement, which took many forms, not the least of which was the Black Panthers and their armed militancy. The other was more general unrest. Now, as a military intelligence officer, even though one was in a domestic office, he had better not have any surprises in his area. In any large urban area, he was courting the possibility that there may be unrest. As the genesis of surveillance by military intelligence, this whole scenario sort of made sense to the American public. But it proceeded without any real guidance.

I went into my first, brief counterintelligence assignment in the Chicago Loop field office in the fall of 1965, and we had some standing collection requests on what was happening, for instance, with a group called the Black Keystone Rangers, because we had military facilities and an Army headquarters

---

107 This instance occurred in the city of Detroit, MI. See David Adams, "Internal Military Intervention in the United States," *Journal of Peace Research*, 32, No. 2 (May 1995), 205.

there. The antiwar movement had not yet blossomed, but it was growing. By 1967 and 1968 it had become a significant concern, not least because a number of National Guard armories had been raided. We had the possibility of protests growing into insurgency. We can look back and judge that to be an overestimation of capabilities, even if not of intentions. However, given the number of Guard armories that had been robbed, an insurgent capability was growing.

The movement that was developing had as its ideology a sort of non-classical Marxism. This was the Mao Era. It was a non-electoral movement, and it was the kind of movement where one could become radicalized at the barricades. Power came out of the barrel of a gun. I think it was one of the reasons why the New Left has such a weak legacy, in terms of the protest movement. It was because the embrace of a culture of protest was alien to America. During the Cold War, we wanted to get foreign peoples behind us. And part of this is that one has to look in the mirror: We had come out of the 1950s and 1960s and we were gangbusters in covert action programs sowing subversion and unrest abroad. And did it not make sense now that maybe our opponents were doing the same thing to us? In my mind, the military took on the internal surveillance role because the FBI could not figure out how to handle it. The Hoover FBI was more accustomed to penetrating the American Communist Party than it was dealing with these young, wild civilians and, since most of us coming into the military service were of these students' age, it was easier for us to penetrate their organizations. Culturally we had quite a lot in common. For many of us, enlisting in military intelligence became a good way for bright kids to satisfy their military obligation in an intellectually stimulating kind of organization. When I was going through my training, there were guys with academic degrees from Princeton, Yale, and places like that. It looked more like the intelligence cadre in WWII than that of today. And it had its appeal because all of us were subject to the draft.

Restraints on Individual Initiative in Intelligence

Consider the motto of the British Special Air Service—"who dares, wins." The implication, whether in operations or in intelligence, is that one has 72 | got to dare to do something different, to dare to do something new, to take risks in order to be successful. U.S. culture extols individual initiative. Allen Dulles would say that our whole business, particularly on the human side, and we could say on the technical side of intelligence too, involves overcoming obstacles to getting the information we need, with our side also having the responsibility of taking initiatives to make it hard for the other side to obtain our own information. We can think of each service wondering, "What are my vulnerabilities?" They will then take certain measures to fix those vulnerabilities, and the winning side is the one that can better assess ways of exploiting vulnerabilities than the other side can invent ways of protecting them. And so there is a premium on imagination, innovation.

In the pre-intelligence reform days of the 1970s, I don't think there were a lot of considerations of law, and of having reference to legal counsel, as we went about our business. One of the ways to map this thought might be to determine trends in the size of the office of General Counsel in the intelligence organization. This would help answer the question: How is intelligence engagement with the rule of law reflected? Let us say that we have a priority intelligence requirement to report on violations of human rights in Guatemala. How can we do that? Probably the best way is to recruit somebody from inside the organization who is committing the alleged violations. We would need to find some way to put them under pressure, under discipline, get them to betray their trust to that organization, and develop greater trust with us. So what we have done, in a technical sense, is recruit someone who is a human rights violator, and put him or her on our payroll. And, because we operate in bureaucracies and information does leak out, we are likely to have a revelation on the front page of a major newspaper that our organization has someone on the payroll who is with the death squads. This points up the value of maintaining continuous consultation with legal counsel in the business today.

What I am most proud of in my years of involvement in Central America is a very systematic and consistent initiative to penetrate the death squads in El Salvador. To do so, we wound up dealing with some awful, awful people. And in the end, we did break the back of the death squads in that period. And in doing so, we gave some positive prospects for a kind of democracy.

Farther down the Isthmus and, in my experience, when we were going after Manuel Noriega in the late 1980s, Congress had restricted the use of funds in Panama, in its frustration over Noriega and our continued military relationship with that country. Thus, we in intelligence had to figure out how to get around this funds restriction in order to succeed in the campaign against Noriega's illegitimate regime, which we all accepted as a noble goal. Even the Congress was in agreement with our aims and considered we were doing a "shared good thing."[108] But my attorney said, as I made some innovative proposals for intelligence actions, "Jon, you guys right now are sitting here preparing to violate the provisions of our treaty with Panama, and I must remind you that treaties have the status of law in this country, and so this is a conspiracy to violate U.S. law."

---

108 Federal Research Division, Library of Congress, *Panama: A Country Study* (Washington, DC: U.S. Government Printing Office, 1989), Ch. 4.

If one has taken an action as a U.S. intelligence officer, and it subsequently is found to be questionable, although everything he did was consistent with the culture in which he was operating, is it the U.S. public, which is represented by intelligence officers through the medium of federal regulations and through Constitutional principles, or the individual officer who has to be held accountable? Lawyers in the Intelligence Community do discourage innovation in the sense that their role is to determine the boundaries of what actions we can take that would still be considered consistent with our laws and system of justice, knowing that the rules vary widely by whatever organizations' cultural rules are being observed. And who else can we ask as we face ethical questions? Do we ask the chaplain? Do we ask our spiritual advisor? Do we ask our attorney? Our attorney should be able to say "yes" or "no." I made my career operating at the edge of the envelope. But I always wanted an attorney around who could confidently tell me where the edge of the envelope was.

When I was growing up, I would hear my father say, "Hey, son, show some initiative. Don't follow the group." We pride ourselves on our individual independence. We celebrate the value of the single person operating alone, carrying out his ideas and being subject to their consequences. At the same time, in the last 15 to 20 years, we have gotten the idea that operating as an intelligence team is equally or more important. This idea is becoming culturally ingrained through training and experience, as we all know that there is no "I" in team. No intelligence officer can really operate independently today. We rely on someone else to do the name traces, to do the biographical check. The hardest thing to do as an intelligence manager, I found, was to give my subordinates free rein to use their initiative—this even in a situation where I had some folks with capacities that literally astounded me in how they defined exercising initiative! And my responsibility overall was to hold them accountable. Accountability has been a great check on incautious initiative. But the countervailing issue is that as a consequence it is the cautious person who rises to the top, which is not the best outcome. My own best work was done for bosses who gave me a lot of freedom to go out and "do things."

The recent discussions surfacing in the press about tensions between CIA Headquarters and the field over the limits of physical abuse or torture in interrogations reflects this problem. We recall the unsettledness in the field following DCI Deutsch's requirement that all potential recruitments must be vetted by headquarters for human rights considerations. This was popularly interpreted to mean that we could not recruit "bad people." I think that was a gross overstatement of the actual instruction but it did create a further caution about how aggressively one could penetrate a death squad or terrorist organization. Headquarters approval was not a given. As we joked then, "Where there is a will, there is also a won't."

A Weakness of U.S. Intelligence Culture: Impatience

Of greater concern than balancing initiative and accountability, certainly in the human source intelligence (HUMINT) realm, is a dreadful impatience, which is also a part of U.S. culture—we seem incapable of waiting long enough to see our operations develop carefully and productively. As a national HUMINT official, I was continuously frustrated when my superiors said that we had to focus on a particular issue, and then they wanted a report back in a week on the progress made! Well, one cannot do HUMINT that way—nor by using a 90-day production plan. On the other hand, can we justify a system that would give us fully five years to develop an operation?

How would we penetrate an Islamist extremist group today? Well, think about all the complications. And then we think, "Well, OK, I have a five-year plan to do this." Along the way we are going to experience a normal, shifting assignment schedule, and two years later there will be little or none of the team continuity necessary for a dedicated operations group. Our colleagues in other countries may play a better game in that regard. We are so subject to a cultural impatience within our bureaucracies that we seem unable to make the individual decisions that would set some people apart and give full play to their long-range initiative. Further, in an open assignment system where individual employees enjoy the ability to choose their own assignments to a great degree, our ability to grow hand-picked people who will come to "act like us" will be limited.

An interesting issue is "Can we isolate an intelligence institution from the general social changes taking place around it?" We can look back to the halcyon days for HUMINT in the United States, when our system was largely an old-boy network in which a HUMINT professional was grown by a master or patron, and assignments abetted and guided the apprenticeship. Now, the usual two-year or three-year assignments that follow a calendar period do not at the same time follow an operational period. Even when one is involved in a sensitive operation, he or she can easily be pulled back to take a course on travel vouchers that is required of all personnel. And that is the nature of large, bureaucratic organizations. Bureaucratic entanglements remain difficult to transcend even for intelligence services. Of course, this situation is certainly not unique to the U.S. cultural scene, but that does not lessen the negative impact that bureaucracy imparts to the improvement of intelligence work.

When I was heading the National Human Requirements Tasking Center, I would ask any audience, professional or academic, "Who are the principal intelligence collectors for the U.S. government on foreign cultural, social, political, and economic affairs that produce most of the intelligence necessary for the conduct of our foreign affairs and national security policy planning?" Each time, without hesitation, most people would say CIA. But no, the principal intelligence collector for the U.S. Government abroad is the Foreign Service of the United States. On any given day its input probably accounts for 60 or 70 percent of the President's Daily Brief. And yet, the members of the Foreign Service will not recognize this. They think of what they do simply as reporting, and they are very proud of that role. In recent years, unfortunately, this role has for various reasons been reduced in a way that I think has had a terrible impact on our understanding of the world abroad. With all of the talk about our needing more HUMINT, I would invest first in the Foreign Service rather than the intelligence agencies per se to address that deficit.[109] In my career, I saw the potential for a perfect complementarity of Foreign Service and Intelligence Community reporting, although it has never been managed well by bureaucrats at the national level.

We live in a world in which there are far more mysteries than there are secrets. Mystery is teased out by good detective work, and that often stems from having people who are well plugged into local circumstances, who can talk with host-country people and display cultural sensitivity, thereby not placing people into incompatible or compromising positions. Therefore, I think what we most need out in the world are good Foreign Service officers. And I remember a whole cast of individuals who, I would hold, have been really good.

But there is a slice of information, especially in the realm of uncovering foreign intentions and policies, that we are not going to get through normal investigation, even using the skills of the Foreign Service Officer. And there we need the capabilities of a clandestine service. For that small slice, we could orchestrate resources in the field to maximize our coverage—and there ought to be a natural complementarity to it. Although clandestine and overt collectors may dress the same and look the same, each does operate with a completely different ethos. Decisions can wisely be made at the national level

---

109 In a Landon Lecture at Kansas State University, Secretary of Defense and former Director of Central Intelligence Robert Gates on 26 November 2007 expressed a similar sentiment in suggesting that the resources of the State Department's Foreign Service be increased, perhaps even at the expense of the Department of Defense. See *http://www.defenselink.mil/speeches/speech.aspx?speechid=1199*.

to more evenly distribute financial resources between the two to prevent too-easy recruitment of Foreign Service officers into the Clandestine Service for financial gain.

In the English-speaking world, my sense is that the British have had far more latitude in the field than we to carry out intelligence assignments. At the headquarters level, too, the fact that the UK foreign intelligence services are all under the Foreign and Commonwealth Office, and they have in their system a permanent under-secretary who takes intelligence issues up with the foreign affairs community, makes them more efficient and perhaps more effective than we are. No country has as fragmented a national intelligence system as we do. All in all, the ease with which diplomats and spooks intermingle differs quite a bit among the different national services. For most countries other than the U.S., I would guess that if we look at the proportion or percentage of their overseas government presence that is made up of intelligence officials, strictly speaking, it is a much smaller proportion than ours.

Postscript

There is a great line I can paraphrase from John Le Carre's *The Russia House*, where, in discussing intelligence work, the character observes, "If enthusiasm and resources provided good intelligence, we would be awash in it." Our technical intelligence means definitely provide a benefit and they have been pretty responsive to our needs. However, if we had the patience and competence to provide long-term direction for a foreign HUMINT program—if we broadened the same sort of planning that we apply now in preparing for a new satellite system, where we have about six years to think about how to make it most productive—then we might be more culturally suited to excel at our profession.

About the Author

Jon A. Wiant started his career in 1962 with service in military intelligence positions, including two tours in Vietnam. His academic preparation included degrees from the University of Colorado and Cornell University, where he was a Danforth Graduate Fellow. He joined the Foreign Service in 1975. His initial assignments focused on Southeast Asia and he developed an international reputation on Golden Triangle drug trafficking. He developed the State Department's first intelligence office looking at transnational threats. In 1982, Wiant became Special Assistant for Special Activities, responsible for bringing policy coordination and oversight of the Reagan Doctrine covert action programs. This continued to be his primary focus as Deputy Director for Intelligence Liaison, and Director for Intelligence Coordination in the Bureau of Intelligence and Research (INR). He subsequently occupied Intelligence Community positions in the Department of Defense, Central Intelligence Agency, and National Security Council and became Deputy Assistant Secretary of State, INR. He served as the State Department's Assistant Inspector General for Security and Intelligence Oversight from 1996 to 2001. He was INR's first recipient of the Director of Central Intelligence's Exceptional Analyst Award. The CIA, the Department of State, and the Department of Defense awarded him numerous medals and citations. On his retirement from the State Department, he received the National Intelligence Distinguished Service Medal from the Director of Central Intelligence. He taught for several years at the National Defense Intelligence College and now lectures on intelligence issues in both government and academic programs. He is an Adjunct Professor at George Washington University.

CANADA'S INTELLIGENCE CULTURE: AN ASSESSMENT

Stéphane Lefebvre

Abstract

In Canada intelligence has traditionally played a rather insignificant role in decision-making. Political leaders, high-level public servants, and diplomats rarely ever mention any interest in intelligence or any use for it. In this chapter, I argue that Canada's intelligence culture, to the extent it can be discerned, exists in the margins of the nation's politics, only coming to the fore at times of perceived major scandals or failures. One of the main reasons for this state of affairs lies in Canada's strategic culture, which privileges ideational factors reflected in international norms and discourses over the relative capability of states. Other reasons include the lack of a critical mass of scholars and journalists to educate Canadian citizens and officials on intelligence issues from multidisciplinary perspectives, and the lack of a national intelligence strategy or long-term vision of the role of intelligence in furthering Canada's national interests. As long as Canada's strategic culture does not see intelligence as a major source of national power, it will remain very difficult for a purely Canadian intelligence culture to emerge beyond the confines of the intelligence community, and for a full-fledged independent national intelligence capability to develop. Post-9/11 changes will need more time to mature to achieve the desired effects.

Introduction

Intelligence contributes to a country's sources of national power. The key leadership figures of the major powers, including the United States, the United Kingdom, France, and Russia, cannot do without it in deliberating issues of strategic significance. This is not the case for Canada, where intelligence has traditionally played a rather insignificant role in decision-making. Political leaders, high-level public servants, and diplomats rarely ever mention any interest in intelligence or any use for it. Tellingly, former Canadian diplomat Peter Johnston disclosed in his memoirs that in 1972 the Clerk of the Privy Council Office (the Deputy Minister to the Prime Minister, Secretary to the Cabinet, and

Head of the Public Service) questioned why the country was spending money on intelligence, what intelligence was, and whether it was needed. Two studies were commissioned back-to-back to answer the Clerk's concerns, both concluding, after consultations with London and Washington, that spending money on Canada's intelligence capabilities was money well spent after all.[110]

This example vividly illustrates the argument often put forward by Canadian intelligence practitioners and academics that their country does not have much of an intelligence culture, if one can be discerned after all. One of the main reasons for this state of affairs lies in Canada's strategic culture, which privileges ideational factors reflected in international norms and discourses over any serious attention to the relative capability of states, from whence would emerge the concepts of international threats and opportunities which are central to an intelligence culture.[111] In this chapter I will thus discuss Canada's strategic culture as it provides the necessary context to assess the place of intelligence in Canada. The way Canadians are, their symbols (e.g., the beaver, the Royal Canadian Mounted Police, hockey), myths (e.g., Canada as a peacekeeping nation), and metaphors (e.g., honest broker, middle power, counterweight) with respect to foreign affairs and defense, all predispose Canadians to see intelligence in a particular light.[112] Canada's strategic culture, some would quickly argue,[113] is itself ill-defined, because the country's strategic interests are poorly understood by politicians, and to civil servants are second to the promotion and projection of Canadian values abroad. This is compounded by the fact that by and large, as historian Jack Granatstein has noted, "Canada is a nation without much sense of its history, and myths inevitably flourish where the facts are not taught, or are willfully forgotten or easily ignored."[114]

---

110 Peter Johnston, *Cooper's Snoopers and Other Follies: A Memoir About Spies, Diplomats and Other Rascals* (Victoria, Trafford Publishing, 2002), pp. 108-109.

111 In other words, I argue that in the Canadian context, ideas, or ideational factors (which refer to variables such as political culture, beliefs, perceptions, identity, international norms, and domestic norms), have greater cultural significance than even primary material factors (such as capabilities, alliance patterns, the balance of military power, economic resources, etc.). For an overview of the role of ideas in international affairs, see Colin Hay, *Political Analysis: A Critical Introduction* (Basingstoke: Palgrave, 2002).

112 See David Haglund, "What Good Is Strategic Culture? A Modest Defence of an Immodest Concept," paper presented at the annual meeting of the International Studies Association (Montreal, 17 March 2004), pp. 18, 23-26.

113 The point is forcefully argued in Scot Robertson, "Years of Innocence and Drift: The Canadian Way of War in the Post-Cold War Era," in *The Canadian Way of War: Serving the National Interest*, edited by Colonel Bernd Horn (Toronto: Dundurn Press, 2006), pp. 359-368.

114 J.L. Granatstein, "The peacekeeping myth: 'Canadians keep the peace; Americans fight wars,' goes the cliché," *The National Post*, January 31, 2007, p. A19.

Canada's National Identity

Today, Canada's traditional national identity (French-English and Catholic-Protestant, often in a tense relationship)[115] is being redefined by increasing cultural, linguistic, ethnic, and religious diversity. The results of the 2001 census show that Canada does not represent an homogenous people,[116] suggesting that what is transcending these multiple diversities is a shared civic identity based on a set of values, connections for points of commonality (through infrastructure, interaction and sectoral collaboration programs—e.g., institutions like the Canadian Broadcasting Corporation, the health care system, etc.), and a culture that accepts differences, all framed and promoted in large part by the federal government. Core values, the key component of Canada's national identity, revolve around the notions of diversity, peace, equality, fairness, and democracy.[117] Diversity, embraced by a majority of Canadians, is embodied in major pieces of federal legislation, including the *Charter of Rights and Freedom*, the *Official Languages Act*, the *Canadian Multiculturalism Act*, and the *Employment Equity Act*. In 2004 a majority of Canadians tended to see Canada first as a multicultural federation, with only 20 percent recognizing the country as a multinational entity with three founding nations (French, English and Aboriginal).[118] In this context, the building of a national identity based on ethnicity is an exercise that has faded into the past, replaced by the idea that Canada is not an ethnic nation, but a civic nation whose social contract is anchored in the *Charter of Rights and Freedom* and in multiculturalism.[119] Given the foregoing, it should not come as a surprise that a majority of Canadians (three in five), notwithstanding the acuity of the terrorist threat, oppose the practice of "ethnic profiling" by security and intelligence agencies. However, of those opposing such profiling, 34 percent do so on moral grounds and 17 percent because they consider such an approach to security ineffective, suggesting lingering tensions between the need to feel safe and tolerance.[120]

---

115 Robert Bothwell, *The Penguin History of Canada* (Toronto: Penguin Canada, 2006), p. 435.

116 For instance, nearly a fifth of Canada's population does not speak either French or English, the two official languages; Canadians trace their origins to no less than 249 ethnocultural groups; and 85 percent of Canadians associate with 33 different world religions. Joanna Anneke Rummens, "Diversity, Identity and Belonging," *Canadian Diversity*, Vol. 3, No. 2, Spring 2004, pp. 39-42.

117 Erin Tolley, "National Identity and the 'Canadian Way': Values, Connections and Culture," *Canadian Diversity*, Vol. 3, No. 2, Spring 2004, pp. 11-15.

118 Jack Jedwab, "The Myth of Canada as a Multinational Federation," *Canadian Diversity*, Vol. 3, No. 2, Spring 2004, p. 21.

119 Chantal Bernier, "Mon pays ce n'est pas un pays, c'est une idée...," *Canadian Diversity*, Vol. 3, No. 2, Spring 2004, pp. 16-18.

120 Doug Fischer, "Many Canadians OK with racial profiling," *The Windsor Star*, September 9, 2006, p. A6.

A small power before the Second World War, Canada emerged from that conflict as an active participant in world affairs. Adopting the mantra of "middle power," it divested itself of much of its military assets—Canada was then the third largest force among Allies—as a conscious move toward relying on influence rather than strict material power (economic and military) to achieve its international objectives. Collective security through international cooperation and organizations became the cornerstone of the country's approach to security in the belief that security at home begins with security abroad. This approach was reflected, in particular, in Canada's foreign intelligence arrangements on signals intelligence (the UK-USA Security Agreement)[121] and defense intelligence arrangements with close allies (for instance in NATO, NORAD and among Anglophone allies—CANUKUS and AUSCANUKUS).

That on some issues, sometimes, Canada achieved a level of influence exceeding its capabilities is not in doubt. However, as Jennifer Welsh argues, this was mainly due to Canada's ability to use processes and tactics to effect, and not because of Canada's ability to muster the necessary material capacity to make things happen.[122] The point should be well taken, as influence does not come from what one says, but from the capabilities one brings to the table.[123] Indeed, according to Welsh, in the post-9/11 context the notion of "middle power" has lost its luster, and to young Canadians is akin to settling for mediocrity. A 2005 survey by Ipsos-Reid for the Canada Institute of the Woodrow Wilson International Center and the Canada Institute on North American Issues gives credence to her views, as 56 percent of Canadians thought that their country is a weak force in world affairs. But this is in contradiction with another poll conducted the preceding year in which 76 percent of Canadians agreed with the statement that, "Canada is a significant player in world affairs."[124] These two polls suggest that Canadians have only the faintest idea of Canada's place in the world, and of its ability and capacity to bring about change and to act in its own interest. It is generally safe to argue that Canadians have little interest in foreign policy and that their views on foreign policy issues are fragmented.[125]

121 See Jeffrey T. Richelson and Desmond Ball, *The Ties That Bind: Intelligence Cooperation Between the UKUSA Countries* (Boston: Allen & Unwin, 1985).

122 Jennifer Welsh's response in *What Is a Canadian: Forty-Three Thought-Provoking Responses*, edited by Irvin Studin (Toronto: McClelland & Stewart, 2006), p. 255.

123 Roy Rempel, *Dreamland: How Canada's Pretend Foreign Policy Has Undermined Sovereignty* (Montreal & Kingston: McGill-Queen's University Press, 2006), p. 15.

124 Ipsos-Reid, *A Public Opinion Survey of Canadians and Americans*, Final Report (May 2005), p. 7.

125 William Hogg, "Plus ça change: Continuity and Culture in Foreign Policy White Papers," *International Journal*, Vol. 59, No. 3, Summer 2004.

This "large-scale ambivalence and lack of understanding about the nature of power and the sources of real influence in international affairs"[126] among Canadians has allowed post-World War II Liberal governments to pursue a foreign policy focused on Canadian values and the notion that "multilateralism must be Canada's primary source of moral authority in international affairs,"[127] no matter what Canada's national interests are in terms of directly benefiting ordinary Canadians. Conservative governments have had enormous difficulty reversing this pattern—including enhancing Canada's material capacity to be a force in the world—which has led over time to a need to differentiate Canada from the United States, and decisions that some would argue are counter to Canada's interests (e.g., the refusal to participate in U.S. missile defense although Canada would be directly affected by any strategic missile attack on the United States).

That Canada "is not a noted leader in a single domain of global affairs or international public policy,"[128] despite its geographical and resource attributes, is clearly baffling to many. For political scientist Thomas Homer-Dixon, this can be explained by the unwillingness of Canadians "to face the reality of our second-rate performance in so many areas, and to do something about it. We are too comfortable being average, even mediocre. We are too happy in our complacency, and too sure in our self-righteousness."[129] To no avail, Canada's diplomats continue to hold the belief that Canada is effective on the international scene because of its "middle power" status[130] as was the case during the Second World War when Canada readily recognized it was not a great power and acted accordingly in the pursuit of the country's interest.[131]

Canadians and the United States

In his diaries written during an eight-year stint (1981-1989) as Canada's ambassador to the United States, Allan Gotlieb candidly remarked that Canadian foreign affairs officials were largely anti-American and that there was little hope of changing their mindset as they spent their time focused on dif-

---

126 This argument is fully developed and empirically supported in Rempel, Dreamland: How Canada's Pretend Foreign Policy Has Undermined Sovereignty. The quote is from p. 5.

127 Rempel, Dreamland: How Canada's Pretend Foreign Policy Has Undermined Sovereignty, p. 68.

128 Thomas Homer-Dixon's response in What Is a Canadian, p. 9.

129 Thomas Homer-Dixon's response in What Is a Canadian, p. 9.

130 William Hogg and Andrew F. Johnson, "Canadian Foreign Policy and the Middle East: Theory and Practice," paper presented at the annual meeting of the International Studies Association (San Diego, March 2006), p. 3.

131 Bothwell, The Penguin History of Canada, p. 360.

ferentiating Canadian from American policies.[132] The views of Canada's diplomats and leaders are not necessarily out of synchronization with the Canadian population at large. Anti-Americanism in Canada today indeed appears to be a defining feature of being Canadian, at the same time as Canadians are avid consumers of U.S. culture and consumer products.

Barbara Ann Allen captures well the attitude of Canadians toward the United States when she writes that, "Canadians often have a rather insular view of themselves. Despite being an immigrant country, there is a sense that we can function in a bubble, interacting with the United States in terms of trade and claiming the benefits, and only committed in terms of defence when it suits us. Canadians criticize the U.S. for their apparent lack of understanding of Canada, and at the same time often claim some kind of passive moral superiority."[133] According to a 2006 Ipsos-Reid survey for the Canada Institute of the Woodrow Wilson International Center and the Canada Institute on North American Issues, 58 percent of Canadians thought of the United States as Canada's closest friend and ally (53 percent in 2005 and 60 percent in 2002), while 63 percent (60 percent in 2005 and 56 percent in 2002) of Americans identified the United Kingdom as the U.S.'s best friend and ally, and only 17 percent Canada (14 percent in 2005 and 18 percent in 2002). In matters of security and intelligence, there is no closer friend and ally of Canada than the United States. Geography, similar personality cultures, a history of working together, and similar security challenges make them natural intelligence allies. The recent Canadian Commission of Inquiry into the Actions of Canadian Officials in Relation to Maher Arar, a Canadian citizen who was shipped by U.S. authorities from New York to Syria and subsequently tortured there, is unlikely to affect the solid foundations of the Canada-U.S. intelligence partnership over the long term, although adjustments on the sharing of intelligence will be required on the Canadian side to ensure that no faulty intelligence is passed on. The impact of the Commission on Inquiry on public opinion is already fading, according to an August 2006 survey showing that 48 percent of Canadians were in support of closer cooperation with the United States in the war against terrorism.[134]

---

132 Paul Gessell, "Foreign Affairs Rife with Anti-Americanism: Gotlieb," The Ottawa Citizen, November 29, 2006, p. A1. See Allan Gotlieb, The Washington Diaries 1981-1989 (Toronto: McClelland & Stewart, 2006).

133 Barbara Ann Allen, "Like a Sub Adrift: Defence Policy as a Litmus Test for the Martin Government," in How Ottawa Spends 2005-2006: Managing the Minority, edited by G. Bruce Doern (Montreal and Kingston: McGill-Queen's University Press, 2005), p. 60.

134 Max Harrold, "Quebecers not too worried about terror attack," The Gazette (Montreal), September 6, 2006, p. A11.

Canadians and National Defense

That foreign policy provides the framework within which defense policy is formulated is now accepted practice in Canada, but it was not always so. Defense reviews, very much like foreign policy reviews, have been conducted on an ad hoc basis (in 1964, 1971, 1987, 1992, 1994, 2005) and certainly "did not result in an encompassing methodical approach to formulating lasting and durable defense plans that were in keeping with foreign policy."[135] Instead, they largely reflected "the preferences of the prime minister of the day."[136]

Many Canadians now share the simplistic views that Canada only uses military force altruistically, although in the post-Cold War era Canada's armed forces have been used in a variety of missions other than peacekeeping, albeit with a tactical rather than a strategic focus. In doing so, costs, liabilities and casualties have to be kept to a minimum, in line with the risk-averse approach to foreign security problems exhibited by politicians.[137]

Despite a rich military history and solid performances in wars, today Canadians are not overwhelmingly willing to entertain huge budgets for their military or see them engaged in operations where they must use force to impose order.[138] For example, the belief that legal arguments are sufficient to counter claims affecting Canada's national interest is still pervasive among Canadians. When asked in a February 2007 survey whether troops should be deployed to assert Canada's sovereignty over the Arctic, only 18 percent of Canadians supported that option, the majority, 52 percent, supporting the notion that Canada should do so through legal authority.[139]

As Barbara Ann Allen explains:

Canadians continue to believe that despite a much weakened military we hold a more than proportional claim to influence on the world stage—a claim stemming from a long since past stellar peacekeeping record. But traditional peacekeeping is not what is needed in the current environment. Though Canadians are patriotic, when push comes to shove, Canadians as citizens are often not willing to back

---

135 Howard G. Coombs and Richard Goette, "Supporting the Pax Americana: Canada's Military and the Cold War," in The Canadian Way of War, p. 268.

136 Allen, "Like a Sub Adrift," p. 61.

137 Bernd Horn, "Introduction," in The Canadian Way of War, pp. 11-16.

138 This is the case with Canada's current mission in Afghanistan. The Economist captured the mood well: "Canadians are nowadays queasy about having an army that actually fights. Most would prefer their soldiers to do pleasanter things, like doling out food, rebuilding shattered villages or donning blue helmets for traditional UN peacekeeping." See "Accentuating the positive," The Economist, Vol. 382, No. 8518, March 3, 2007, p. 46.

139 The Ottawa Sun, February 23, 2007, p. 7.

up the belief in robust defense with the tough choices—trade-offs and subsequent sacrifices needed either through less generous social spending or the higher taxation that a comprehensive rebuilding of the military requires. It is much easier to let the United States take care of it. In defense terms Canadians are often classic "free riders."[140]

During the Cold War, Canadian participation in military missions was focused on tactical-level operations. The resulting mindset has proven difficult to change within the context of complex post-Cold War missions, where tactical decisions often have disproportionate impact at the operational and strategic levels. Canadian army commanders, responding to this new reality, are now putting a premium on intelligence that never existed during the Cold War.[141] Military intelligence is now valued more than ever, but this creates challenges for intelligence officers and operators who now need to adapt and respond to new requirements spanning the tactical, operational, and strategic realms.[142] This is compounded, according to Canadian military intelligence officers, by a doctrine still largely informed by its Cold War predecessors and in need of a major overhaul.[143]

Of note, Canada's military intelligence branch has a long history going back a century, of which, unfortunately, little is known in the public and academia at large.[144] Contrary to the United States, Canada's military intelligence effort, either at the strategic, operational or tactical level, is small (less than a thousand personnel), confined within the bureaucratic structure of the Department of National Defence and within military units (brigade-level and below), and seldom under media scrutiny. That the branch lost its identity through its

---

140 Allen, "Like a Sub Adrift," p. 60.

141 The 2003 Canadian Forces' Joint Intelligence Doctrine manual recognizes intelligence as an "essential component of military capability." Department of National Defence, Joint Intelligence Doctrine, B-GJ-005-200/FP-000, May 21, 2003, p. 1-1.

142 Lieutenant-Colonel Daniel Villeneuve, "A Study of the Changing Face of Canada's Army Intelligence," Canadian Army Journal, Vol. 9, No. 2, Summer 2006, pp. 24-25.

143 See, inter alia, Villeneuve, "A Study of the Changing Face of Canada's Army Intelligence," p. 30; Captain Lisa Elliott, "Finding a Balance: A Study of the Canadian Army's Approach to Human Intelligence in an Asymmetric Environment," unpublished master's degree thesis (Kingston: Royal Military College of Canada, April 2005), as republished in Major Harold A. Skaarup, Out of Darkness—Light: A History of Canadian Military Intelligence, Volume 3, 1998-2005 (New York: iUniverse, Inc., 2005), p. 339.

144 The literature on Canada's military intelligence history is limited to a few major works, including Major S. R. Elliott, Scarlet to Green: Canadian Army Intelligence 1903-1963 (Toronto: Canadian Intelligence and Security Association, 1981); Major Harold A. Skaarup, Out of Darkness-Light: A History of Canadian Military Intelligence, 3 volumes. Volume 1, Pre-Confederation to 1982; Volume 2, 1983-1997; Volume 3, 1998-2005 (New York: iUniverse, Inc., 2005); and Wesley Wark, "The Evolution of Military Intelligence in Canada," Armed Forces & Society, Vol. 16, No. 1, Fall 1989, pp. 77-98. Specialized government and professional military publications have carried a small number of articles over the years, some of which are reprinted in Skaarup's three-volume series.

absorption by a newly created security branch (coupling police and intelligence functions) in 1968 has long been forgotten. It took no less than three formal studies affirming that police and intelligence functions are clearly distinct to convince the military hierarchy to recreate a distinct intelligence branch in 1982 (on the 40th anniversary of the creation of the original Canadian Intelligence Corps).[145] Prior to the terrorist attacks of 11 September 2001 (9/11), and Canada's subsequent military deployment to Afghanistan, the intelligence branch was reportedly suffering from neglect, its intelligence collection capabilities eroding and experienced personnel leaving to retirement or the private sector. Since then, it has been reorganized, obtained additional funding, increased its personnel (both military and civilian), established the Canadian Forces School of Military Intelligence (in 2002), and is fully engaged in providing intelligence support to deployed contingents.[146] Military intelligence professionals are, in the context of the global war on terrorism, widely considered to be of equal importance to the operations staff. This marks a cultural shift in the Canadian Forces. In fact, the latest issue of the Canadian Forces' operations doctrine states unequivocally that intelligence is "command led," requiring the Commander to drive the intelligence process and have a solid understanding of it.[147] To inform the public about military intelligence and intelligence issues generally, the Canadian Forces Intelligence Branch Association has developed a dedicated web page (*http://www.intbranch.org/home-e.html*). Line reserve intelligence companies also maintain official web pages where they describe what they do, albeit mostly for recruiting purposes.[148]

9/11

Canada's senior political leadership was taken aback and surprised by the events of 11 September 2001. The prime minister's senior policy adviser recognized that the terrorist threat posed by Al Qaeda was not on the government's radar the previous day.[149] This suggests that the prime minister and his close circle of advisers had either not read or heeded the threat assessments on

---

145 Major James D. Godefroy, "Supporting Operations–A Proud Record of Service," in Skaarup, Out of Darkness, Vol. 3, pp. 137-138.

146 See David A. Charters, "The Future of Military Intelligence Within the Canadian Forces," Canadian Military Journal, Winter 2001-2002, pp. 47-52; and Skaarup, Out of Darkness, Vol. 3, chapters on the years 2001 to 2005.

147 Department of National Defence, Canadian Forces Operations, B-GJ-005-300/FP-000, November 5, 2004, p. 15-1.

148 The military's signals branch is also involved in intelligence gathering through the Canadian Forces Signals Intelligence Operations Centre (CFSOC), which is part of the Department of National Defence's Information Management Group (URL: *http://www.img.forces.gc. ca/org/cfiog/cfsoc_e.asp*).

149 Goldenberg, The Way It Works, p. 264.

international terrorism, and specifically Al Qaeda, produced by the Canadian Security Intelligence Service (CSIS) over the preceding years. This is indicative of the lack of an intelligence culture in the senior levels of government. In its 2001-2002 report, the Security Intelligence Review Committee (SIRC), the review body for CSIS, indeed noted that the CSIS investigation of Al Qaeda and Sunni Islamic terrorism was complex, aggressive, and of long standing. The Committee further concluded that CSIS had advised government of the threat posed by Al Qaeda and Sunni Islamic terrorism in a timely and comprehensive fashion. Although it was not aware of the specifics of 9/11 and did not predict it, "the Service [CSIS] clearly was aware of the potential for Al Qaeda-inspired terrorist attacks of some kind and communicated this information to the appropriate bodies in government."[150] Today, CSIS produces specific *Intelligence Briefs for the Prime Minister*, which are forwarded through the Clerk of the Privy Council.[151]

The government quickly recognized the necessity to address the new security situation brought to the fore by 9/11 to preserve commerce with the United States. Because it lacked a national security policy framework or doctrine to respond, the Liberal government did so through ad hoc measures while pondering how a new focus on security would affect its immigration and multicultural policies.[152] The measures it eventually took in response to 9/11 took several forms, from additional budgetary allocations to CSIS, the Communications Security Establishment (CSE–Canada's signals intelligence organization); and the Royal Canadian Mounted Police (RCMP–Canada's federal law enforcement agency) to the adoption of major pieces of legislation, including the *Anti-Terrorism Act* in 2001 and the *Public Safety Act* in 2004 (creating, among other things, new terrorism offences, terrorist financing offences, and new police powers). In its legislative approach, the government was cautious in balancing the

---

150 Security Intelligence Review Committee, SIRC Report 2001-2002: An Operational Audit of the Canadian Security Intelligence Service (Ottawa: Public Works and Government Services Canada, 2002), p. 7.

151 One such Brief obtained by the National Post newspaper was on "Radicalization and Jihad in the West." It was forwarded by the Clerk to the Prime Minister on June 20, 2006, and returned by the Prime Minister's officer on June 29. There is no indication that the Brief was read by the Prime Minister. Although classified Secret/Canadian Eyes Only, the Brief was very general, lacking in detail and analysis, and written in a very simplistic tone. While it noted the existence of academic research on Islamic radicalization, the Brief did not reflect the richness and contentious aspect of this literature, suggesting instead that "further investigations and research must be carried out [...]." A copy of the Brief was posted at URL: *http://www.canada.com/nationalpost/pdf/pm_brief_new.pdf* on March 20, 2007.

152 Goldenberg, The Way It Works, pp. 265, 267; Reg Whitaker, "Made in Canada? The New Public Safety Paradigm," in How Ottawa Spends 2005-2006: Managing the Minority, edited by G. Bruce Doern (Montreal and Kingston: McGill-Queen's University Press, 2005), p. 78. Canada's first National Security Policy was published in April 2004 (*http://www.pco-bcp.gc.ca/docs/Publications/NatSecurnat/natsecurnat_e.pdf*) and updated in April 2005 (*http://www.pco-bcp.gc.ca/docs/ministers/deputypm/secure_e.pdf*).

protection of civil rights with the need for greater security and more powerful investigative and enforcement mechanisms, and considered that its new measures were Charter of Rights and Freedom-proof, and on solid legal grounds. They were not. Already three subsections of the *Security of Information Act*, and the definition of terrorism in the *Criminal Code*, all enacted through the *Anti-Terrorism Act*, have been declared unconstitutional, respectively for restricting freedom of expression including freedom of the press and for infringing the liberty of religion, expression, and association.[153] Separate from these measures, Canada's security certificate provisions (in the *Immigration and Refugee Protection Act*), which allow for the detention and removal of foreign nationals posing a security threat, were recently struck down as well, but were to remain on the books for an additional year so as to allow government to bring about the Supreme Court's suggested corrections.[154]

By the end of 2003, the government had announced major bureaucratic changes to the security and intelligence community, which showed, in the words of Reg Whitaker, "an overarching concern for the *integration and coordination of government machinery* in the national security area, and for a more *comprehensive and inclusive definition of threats to security* that goes beyond terrorism alone."[155] The changes included creating the position of National Security Adviser to the Prime Minister to improve national security and public safety coordination and policy formulation, foster better inter-agency cooperation, and coordinate integrated threat assessments, and the Department of Public Safety and Emergency Preparedness (PSEPC) to ensure coordination across all federal departments and agencies responsible for national security and the safety of Canadians. To encourage information-sharing and cooperation among organizations that collect and analyze intelligence, the government activated in October 2004 an Integrated Threat Assessment Centre (ITAC) within CSIS.[156] While it is too early to assess whether these changes have made a difference in ensuring the security of Canada and its allies, anecdotal evidence communicated to the author in confidence suggests that they are works in progress enduring growing pains.

---

153 See O'Neill v. Canada (Attorney General), 2006 CanLII 35004 (Ontario Superior Court of Justice), December 18, 2006, at *http://www.canlii.org/on/cas/onsc/2006/2006onsc16405. html*; and R. v. Khawaja, Ontario Superior Court of Justice, Case 04-G30282, October 24, 2006, at *http://www.theglobeandmail.com/special/audio/Rutherford.pdf*.

154 See the Supreme Court decision, Charkaoui vs. Canada (Citizenship and Immigration), 207 SCC 9, at *http://scc.lexum.umontreal.ca/en/2007/2007scc9/2007scc9.html*.

155 Whitaker, "Made in Canada?" p. 80.

156 See Whitaker, "Made in Canada?" p. 88; CSIS Backgrounder No. 13 on ITAC at *http://www.csis-scrs.gc.ca/en/newsroom/backgrounders/backgrounder13.asp*. More details on PSEPC are available at *http://www.psepc-sppcc.gc.ca/index-en.asp* and on the NSA at *http://www.pco-bcp.gc.ca/*.

Canada's Strategic Culture as Context for the Security and Intelligence Community

The foregoing suggests that Canada's strategic culture is heavily influenced by ideational factors first and foremost, and is in need of a coherent strategic framework to make national security decisions in the national interest. Canada's diplomats remain deluded that the words of a "middle power" can influence the behavior of major powers. The military has to contend with difficult missions that few among the public understand while catching up from years of procurement neglect. The national security apparatus is only starting to work in a more coordinated and cooperative fashion while facing a host of legal challenges to its post-9/11 legislation. Parliamentarians know little about national security (especially its intelligence component) and have little interest, with a few notable exceptions in the Senate, in discussing it, unless there is an alleged scandal they could exploit to attack the political party forming the government.[157] This being said, since 9/11 there has been an increase in media coverage of intelligence issues and in student demands for more university courses on intelligence in a number of academic disciplines (law, political science, and history). Anecdotal evidence (ad hoc discussions with professors and students) suggests that these demands are largely fueled by all the reporting on the alleged misuse of U.S. intelligence, such as the use of torture to gather intelligence, stories of rendition (including that of Canadian Maher Arar mentioned above), and concerns that rights are not sufficiently balanced with the need for security.

If there is little evidence of a strong national security focus across the public and private sector in Canada, there is even less evidence of an intelligence culture.[158] Intelligence is rarely used in strategic decision-making and few senior officials appear to make any regular use of it. If they do, they are not saying so to Canadians, unless it is to reassure them they are safe when threats are reported. For example, Transport Canada officials have noted that intelligence is in fact important to the development of adequate security measures in the areas of rail, air, and maritime transportation.[159] The assertion, however, that there is "in the Canadian government, media and public at large, an appalling lack of understanding of the true nature of the intelli-

---

157 Whitaker, "Made in Canada?" p. 89

158 Brigadier General (Retd) James S. Cox, "Canada Needs a National Security Intelligence Policy," April 2004, posted at *http://www.ccs21.org/articles/related/2004/cox_national_security_intell_apr04.pdf.*

159 For example, see the frequent mention of intelligence in an official question-and-answer exchange at *http://www.tc.gc.ca/vigilance/sep/passenger_protect/Q&A.htm.*

gence function,"[160] remains valid. A case in point is an early 2005 survey conducted by Ekos, which stunningly revealed that 31 percent of Canadians (46 percent in the French province of Quebec) had never heard of CSIS, Canada's main intelligence agency created from the RCMP Security Service in 1984. In the same survey, 67 percent wrongly thought that CSIS officers could arrest or detain individuals involved in activities that threaten national security; 32 percent that CSIS officers could carry handguns (32 percent did not know one way or another); 63 percent that CSIS was collecting information on protesters against the government regardless of whether or not they have violent intentions; while 82 percent agreed that it was important to have an organization like CSIS to investigate threats to national security.[161] Another case in point is the candid admission of Margaret Bloodworth, Canada's current National Security Advisor. Reflecting on her years as Coordinator of Security and Intelligence in the Privy Council Office between 1994 and 1996, she commented that "in the 1990s, the security and intelligence sector was not very well understood, either within government or outside. There's no question that Canada has never really had an 'intelligence culture.'"[162]

To develop an understanding and appreciation of the role and functions of intelligence in a democratic society like Canada, education will be essential. But even there, despite more students' demands for courses[163] and media interest in conferences dealing with intelligence matters, there is little hope that an intelligence culture can be nurtured from within academia at the moment. At the 2006 conference of the Canadian Association for Security and Intelligence Studies (CASIS), Carleton University professor Martin Rudner commented that Canada's academic community had little interest in studying intelligence. To wit, he noted the following statistics: out of 530 conference attendees, there were only 20 academics, of whom only 8 were involved in intelligence studies. Collectively, Canada's 79 universities were offering a grand total of 9 courses related to intelligence. Even more startling, he added that, as a matter of principle, the board of governors of the Social Sciences and Humani-

---

160 Brigadier General (Retd) James S. Cox, "The Essence of the Intelligence Function," paper presented at the CDAI-CDFAI 7th Annual Graduate Student Symposium, Royal Military College of Canada, 29-30 October 2004, p. 2.

161 Ekos Research Associates, Inc., Wave 10: Additional CSIS Questions. Part of the Security Monitor 2004 (Ottawa, April 2005). A similar survey conducted six months later by Ekos obtained similar results (plus or minus 3-4 percent).

162 Speaking Notes for Margaret Bloodworth, Deputy Minister of National Defence at the Conference of the Canadian Association for Security and Intelligence Studies (Ottawa, September 27, 2002), p. 3.

163 Canadian Press, "CSIS Aims to Boost Ranks by Recruiting at Canadian Universities," 3 January 2007.

ties Research Council does not favor awarding research grants for intelligence-related research agendas.[164]

In the current bureaucratic framework, intelligence agencies are part of government and are subject, with a few exceptions (for instance, CSIS can act as a separate employer for staffing purposes), to the same rules and oversight and review mechanisms as other departments and agencies. The Auditor General of Canada, the Canadian Human Rights Commission, the Privacy Commissioner, and the Information Commissioner all can, and effectively do, monitor the performance of the intelligence agencies in accordance with their respective mandate. In addition to these general review bodies, there is at least one specific review body for each of Canada's three major intelligence agencies: an Inspector General and Security Intelligence Review Committee (an independent and external review body reporting to parliament) for CSIS; a Communications Security Establishment Commissioner for CSE; and a Commission for Public Complaints Against the RCMP. As a result of the Arar Inquiry, a review of all national security review bodies is underway, which may lead to a new all-encompassing review structure for all departments and agencies involved in national security. No intelligence agency in Canada is thus above the law and each has a legislative basis for its activities.[165] The legal provisions and legal framework within which Canada's intelligence community operates would suggest that one aspect of a Canadian intelligence culture is that it is characterized by legality. However, it was only in 2001 that a legal basis was given to the activities of CSE, about a decade after its very existence was officially acknowledged by government. The respect for the law, along with the fact that in Canada leaks and unauthorized releases of classified information are very rare, suggests that there has long been a tradition of secrecy maintained by the members of the intelligence community.

---

164 Dr. Rudner's comments were reported in Cameron Ortis, Editor, CASIS 2006 International Conference: Report (Ottawa, 26-28 October 2006), p. 28, available at *http://www.casis. ca/french/CASIS-2006-FINAL-REPORT.pdf.*

165 The Canadian Security Intelligence Service Act for CSIS (R.S., 1995, c. C-23); the National Defence Act, Part V1 for CSE (R.S., 1985, c. N-5); and the Royal Canadian Mounted Police Act for the RCMP (R.S., 1985, c. R-10), all available on the Justice Canada webpage at *http://laws.justice.gc.ca.*

Because Canada's major intelligence agencies operate under laws within a larger bureaucratic framework, they behave no differently from other federal departments and agencies. They fight for their prerogatives and to protect their turf,[166] and must submit Memoranda to the Cabinet and to the Treasury Board to get major initiatives approved and funded. It is only very recently that significant improvements have been made to the coordination of intelligence requirements[167] and the production of integrated threat assessments. The pre-9/11 stovepipes are being broken slowly through better integration, but the process still has to develop and mature further before optimum efficacy and efficiency are attained. The first-ever National Security Policy, issued in 2004 by a Liberal government, was a good starting point, but the Conservative government elected in 2006 has made no serious mention of it nor has there been an effort to update it. With respect to intelligence, the Policy has not led to a national intelligence strategy looking at reconciling ends and means, whereas it has done so with regard to areas such as transportation security (a Transportation Security Action Plan is expected to be released in 2007) or the response to chemical, biological, radiological, and nuclear incidents.[168] A national intelligence strategy would arguably give "the entire community [...] a guiding vision, strategy, architecture and synergy."[169]

While Canada's national identity is clearly in flux, it is interesting to note the cozy relationships Canadian intelligence agencies have with those of close allies such as the United States, the United Kingdom, Australia, and New Zealand. That they speak the same language is a factor, but more fundamentally, as Brigadier General Cox aptly observes, "[t]he roots of the Canadian intelligence function are embedded in our British heritage and seasoned by our intimate relationship with the US."[170] All draw on liberal political traditions and for all intents and purposes share similar values, differing only on how each can translate them into action. As Canadian intelligence organizations become more diverse in line with employment equity programs, it will be interesting to see whether this "Anglosphere" of agencies will remain as cohesive as it is today.

---

166   CSIS and the RCMP have reportedly squabbled with one another for years, despite denials by their respective senior officials. See Andrew Meyeda, "After Years of Turf Wars, RCMP, CSIS Agree on Truce," The Ottawa Citizen, 27 October 2006.

167   "Of note, it was only in 1991 that, for the first time, the Government of Canada adopted an intelligence directive setting out its priority requirements for foreign intelligence collection." Martin Rudner, "Canada's Communications Security Establishment from Cold War to Globalization," Intelligence and National Security, 16, No. 1 (Spring 2001), p. 114.

168   For a discussion of the National Security Policy and the need for a national security strategy, see Captain (N) Peter Avis, "Government Must Have a Clear End-state Vision," Frontline Security, Issue 1, 2006, pp. 10-13.

169   Cox, "Canada Needs a National Security Intelligence Policy."

170   Cox, "The Essence of the Intelligence Function," p. 9.

My view is that they will as long as they continue to cultivate and maintain the trust they have developed over the past 65-70 years. Incidentally, these and other links seem important to Canadian air travellers, 64 percent of whom in 2006 had confidence that Canadian authorities are receiving good intelligence concerning potential threats to air security (62 percent in 2005 and 56 percent in 2004).[171]

As discussed above, Canada's strategic culture does not revolve around the use of force in international relations, unless it is clearly mandated under international law or in accordance with well-delineated human security principles. This absence of propensity for taking the offensive is reflected in the debate over the creation of a foreign intelligence service. While for a decade intelligence experts have advocated the creation of a Canadian foreign intelligence agency to gather human intelligence abroad beyond that related to threats to Canada, which CSIS is already doing, there has been little concerted movement in that direction. The Conservative Party elected to government in 2006 had promised to do so, but because it is a minority government it is unlikely to push the issue, knowing the negative connotation such a decision would have with many Canadians.[172] Seeing the types of activities the CIA has been accused of since 9/11 (CIA renditions and allegations of torture, FBI abuse of authorities, etc.), many Canadians would conclude that a Canadian foreign intelligence agency would likely fall into the same path due to the offensive and illegal nature of spying abroad. Although all the major powers and several lesser powers have "offensive" intelligence services, it would be beneath Canada, many would argue, to develop a similar capability as it would affect Canada's ability to promote its values abroad and possibly taint its diplomats and other emissaries as possible spies. This attitude is further ammunition to Rempel's assessment that there is ambivalence and lack of understanding among Canadians about the nature of power in the world. The debate on this issue has also highlighted the lobbying CSIS is doing to enhance its responsibility in this area.[173]

Just as defense policy is supposed to flow from foreign policy, certain intelligence policies are subject to consultations with the Minister of Foreign Affairs. This is the case of CSIS's relationships with foreign agencies, which

---

171 Ekos Research Associates Inc., Public Perceptions of Flight Safety and the Security of Air Travel in Canada: Wave V. Final Report (Ottawa, 31 March 2006), pp. 40-41. Of note, those with higher education and income and flying more often were more likely to disagree.

172 For a thorough discussion of the proposal, see Barry Cooper, "CFIS: A Foreign Intelligence Service for Canada", Canadian Defence and Foreign Affairs Institute, November 2007. http://www.cdfai.org/PDF/CFISF.pdf.

173 See Andrew Meyeda, "Conservative's Spy Agency Promise in Limbo," The Ottawa Citizen, 13 February 2007.

cannot be activated unless CSIS consults first with the Minister of Foreign Affairs in accordance with Section 17 of the *CSIS Act*:

> 17. (1) For the purpose of performing its duties and functions under this Act, the Service may,
>
> ...
>
> (b) with the approval of the Minister [of Public Safety and Emergency Preparedness] after consultation by the Minister with the Minister of Foreign Affairs, enter into an arrangement or otherwise cooperate with the government of a foreign state or an institution thereof or an international organization of states or an institution thereof.[174]

In light of 9/11 and the Maher Arar case, such relationships are expected, now more than ever, to take into consideration the human rights record of the prospective partner before a decision is taken. This is in line with Canadian values.

Also in line with Canadian values, intelligence organizations have made serious attempts at reflecting Canada's diversity, and, following government legislation and policy directives, have put in place programs and policies to recruit a higher numbers of representatives from designated groups (women, natives, visible minorities, and the handicapped).

While there may not be much of an intelligence culture to speak of at the national level, an argument can be made that such a culture can be recognized from within the intelligence community itself. This internal culture has its basis in the history of intelligence in Canada, which goes as far back as the time of confederation in 1867, when intelligence duties fell on the lap of the Dominion Police Force.[175] In 1920, all intelligence functions were consolidated within the purview of the RCMP, which had absorbed the Dominion Police Force. In 1984, after a series of wrongdoings and the subsequent recommendations of two commissions (the Mackenzie Royal Commission on security in 1969, and the McDonald Commission of Inquiry into certain activities of the RCMP in 1984), the government decided to uncouple law enforcement and intelligence functions by dissolving the RCMP security service and transferring many of its security service agents to a newly minted civilian service, CSIS (the Department of National Defence had made a similar move two years earlier). As a result, the

| 95

---

174 See *http://www.csis-scrs.gc.ca/en/publications/act/csisact.asp*.

175 A decent historical overview is provided in A New Review Mechanism for the RCMP's National Security Activities, Commission of Inquiry into the Actions of Canadian Officials in Relation to Maher Arar (Ottawa: Minister of Public Works and Government Services, 2006), pp. 23-53.

intelligence community's culture is no longer associated with a law enforcement culture, despite the controversy the uncoupling initially unleashed. The culture of secrecy noted above affected the relationship between the RCMP and CSIS in the years to come, and may have on occasions prevented the sharing of relevant intelligence between them.[176] The relationship between both agencies has incidentally been one of the areas under investigation by the current Commission of Inquiry into the Investigation of the Bombing of Air India Flight 182 (visit *http://www.majorcomm.ca*), which occurred in 1985.

In the aftermath of 9/11, the notion that intelligence analysts across the community are professionals has really taken off, with a Canadian Association of Professional Analysts (CAPIA) blossoming,[177] and a core entry-level training curriculum in intelligence analysis now being offered to all analysts across the community, with further courses being planned for experienced analysts and managers of analysts.[178] In many respects, these two initiatives (largely driven from the bottom up) were necessary because of the growth in personnel experienced by the community, including both core organizations (CSIS, RCMP, National Defence, CSE, and the International Assessment Secretariat located within the PCO) and smaller intelligence players such as the Departments of Transport, Immigration, and others, and the perceived needs to strengthen analytical standards. Despite the impulse given to this initiative by the highly publicized U.S. and British experience with respect to mis-estimating the existence of Iraq's weapons of mass destruction, these two initiatives have gone unnoticed in the Canadian media.

Conclusion

In this paper, I have discussed Canada's strategic culture, its application to foreign and defense matters, and the impact of 9/11, all in order to provide a context within which a Canadian intelligence culture could be examined. At the national level, Canada lacks a clearly identifiable or unique intelligence culture:

- Intelligence is poorly understood and largely unappreciated by most Canadians, including government officials;

176 See Lessons to be Learned: The report of the Honourable Bob Rae, Independent Advisor to the Minister of Public Safety and Emergency Preparedness, on outstanding questions with respect to the bombing of Air India Flight 182 (Ottawa: Air India Review Secretariat, 2005).

177 CAPIA, supported by the Privy Council Office, was "created to promote training and high analytical standards with the Canadian intelligence community and foster networks and information sharing." The Honourable Paul Martin, Privy Council Office 2004-2005 Departmental Performance Report (Ottawa: Privy Council Office, 2005), p. 37.

178 Comments by Privy Council official Monik Beauregard, reported in Cameron Ortis, Editor, CASIS 2006 International Conference: Report (Ottawa, 26-28 October 2006), p. 15, available at *http://www.casis.ca/french/CASIS-2006-FINAL-REPORT.pdf*.

- Intelligence is not strongly embedded in the daily routines of senior political leaders, bureaucrats, and diplomats;
- There is no critical mass of scholars and journalists to educate Canadian citizens and officials on intelligence issues from multidisciplinary perspectives;
- Intelligence is not seen as a serious or important attribute of Canada's national power;
- Intelligence powers are seen as something that must be balanced with Canadian values, in particular civil rights;
- Similar to defense, intelligence capabilities were largely neglected until 9/11 (huge budget and personnel cuts occurred in the early to the mid-1990s);
- Reflective of Canada's broader strategic culture, there is no national intelligence strategy or long-term vision of the role of intelligence in furthering Canada's national interests;
- Top-level decisions related to intelligence matters are ad hoc in nature; and
- The intelligence function in Canada would quickly atrophy without the significant input from key allies such as the United States, the United Kingdom, and Australia.

The intelligence culture that does appear to exist is located within the community itself and consists of the following elements (which, I would contend, are not necessarily unique to Canada):

- Secrecy (leaks and unauthorized releases of classified material are rare);
- Professionalization (solid push for self-improvement across the community of intelligence analysts and at National Defence);
- Affinities and vibrant relationships (bilateral and multilateral) with Anglosphere intelligence communities;
- Increased acceptance of cross-pollination of intelligence officials across agencies post-9/11;
- Diversity (and recognition, in recruitment campaigns, that it represents an asset);
- Dissociation of intelligence from law enforcement;
- Acceptance of review and oversight mechanisms; and
- Strong desire to protect Canadians and allies.

As long as Canada's strategic culture is founded on ideational factors, it will remain very difficult for a purely Canadian intelligence culture to emerge at the national level and a full-fledged independent national intelligence capability to develop. Most government officials do not know what they need from intelligence, why they need it, and how to use it. Integrating intelligence into policymaking will be an arduous process. National security laws, too, are in need of rebuilding and consolidation after the challenges and losses of 2006 and 2007. On the academic side, intelligence studies are difficult and still distrusted by academia and students alike. The enhanced interest seen lately may change this, but the change will be incremental and over a long period. While there are new trends, recent changes will need more time to mature to achieve the desired effects. On the other hand, the intelligence community has its own culture, which is evolving positively in the post-9/11 era. The challenge for anyone trying to better understand it is to do so from the outside rather than the inside. It is hoped that in due time the community would embark on a major effort to highlight its progress and challenges, and further involve academics and other experts in intelligence in its efforts to be better understood.

About the Author

Mr. Stéphane Lefebvre is Section Head—Strategic Analysis at the Centre for Operational Research and Analysis (CORA), Defence Research and Development Canada (DRDC). He has written extensively on intelligence and European security issues. The views expressed in this chapter are his own and do not reflect the official position of the government of Canada or any of its departments and agencies. The author would like to thank Dr. Russell Swenson and Mr. Greg Smolynec for their comments and suggestions on earlier versions of this chapter. Contact: *stephane.Lefebvre@drdc-rddc.gc.ca.*

NATIONAL INTELLIGENCE, MADE IN USA

Bowman H. Miller

To cope with its troubles, America needs something that arguably goes against our national grain—a truly great intelligence service that can operate powerfully, invisibly, legally.[179]

Abstract

U.S. strategic culture reflects a potent mix of ideals and self-interest, and the power and secrecy of its intelligence establishment fit within a society which distrusts both of those traits. This often reluctant world superpower expects nothing less of its costly intelligence establishment than total knowledge and accurate warning of events and trends across the globe. Policy-maker insistence on analytic precision and "no surprises" clarity confronts an analytic community steeped in nuance and enveloped in uncertainties—all of this in a country which also fears an over-abundance of central power among its intelligence and law enforcement bodies, huge as they are. That massive size is also a hindrance to success, given the need for agility, adaptability, and creativity in the face of dispersed transnational threats. Besides facing the enormous challenge of tracking and anticipating the range of perils in a globalizing world, the U.S. intelligence enterprise remains fixated on technological solutions to its problems, and the informed public and Congress demand a more assured return on their expensive intelligence investment. Although failure is a fact of life in business in America and not a disincentive to taking risks, "intelligence failure," in contrast, has become unacceptable and inexcusable, making the intelligence enterprise more conservative than it ought to be.

| 99

---

[179] David Ignatius, "For Hayden, Repair Work at the CIA," *The Washington Post,* 8 November 2006, 27.

Introduction

Individuals and institutions are shaped by the culture[180] into which they are born and in which they live, and the world of collecting and analyzing intelligence[181] is no exception. This essay relates some of America's national myths, generic traits, legends, self-images, and frailties to the ways in which the accumulation and articulation of national intelligence are carried out and to the products of that complex set of processes and players. Cultures have much to do with how we do things and approach issues; thus, they shape both our mental processes and our conclusions, just as each culture's language and vocabulary express ideas, facts, and judgments in unique ways. Linguists have long declared that all meaning is contextual—and cultures are the predominant fabric of that context. It is impossible to divorce the shape of one's attitudes and judgments, of one's interpretation of events and expectations of developments, from the enveloping culture in which all of that thinking, concluding, and relating of facts and ideas occurs.

Isolation Not an Option

With continuous CNN and other news coverage, increasing foreign penetration of U.S. society, and the rising prevalence of Spanish in many areas of the country, being "isolated" or "isolationist" is, if it has any reality at all, primarily an attitudinal truth in today's United States. The country is as multicultural today as it has ever been, even though many find that worrisome, or at least disquieting. Those who worry over declining "homogeneity," such as Samuel Huntington and the late Arthur Schlesinger, actually evince concern over the dilution of the Anglo-Saxon predominance in U.S. social, cultural and political life in the face of continuing immigration, much of it from beyond

---

180 For purposes of this discussion, I will use "culture" to mean all those traits, myths, shared histories and traditions which provide the essential glue and identity of a nation or people, i.e., essentially the behaviors and beliefs of a nation, or, as one author has termed them, the "software of the mind." See Geert Hofstede and Gert Jan Hofstede, Cultures and Organizations: Software of the Mind (New York: McGraw-Hill, 2004). What George Washington described in 1796 still constitutes the essence of America's defining cultural commonalities: "With slight shades of difference, you have the same religion, manners, habits, and political principles." "Washington's Farewell Address 1796," The Avalon Project at Yale Law School. *http://www.yale.edu/lawweb/avalon/washing.htm*, accessed March 20, 2007. See also the classic study of anthropology by Franz Boas, Race, Language and Culture (New York: Macmillan, 1940), in which he notes, inter alia, that "...forms of thought and action which we are inclined to consider as based on human nature are not generally valid, but characteristic of our specific culture (255)." This serves as a constant reminder against mirror-imaging of others, a persistent failing of U.S. national intelligence.

181 The concept of "intelligence" in this discussion, unless otherwise noted, will be taken to denote concealed information belonging to others that is obtained without permission and is maintained in secrecy.

Huntington's "West." Indeed, the perceived threat to "white, Anglo-Saxon, protestant" (WASP) culture explains most of this sensitivity, even if those who harbor it find themselves powerless to check an unmistakable, probably irreversible, trend.[182]

The last half of the 20th century thrust America into a leading, institution-forming role in world affairs—as "witnesses at the creation," in Secretary of State Dean Acheson's terminology.[183] However, more than just witnesses, U.S. leaders in government, non-government organizations, business, education, science and the arts all took on roles in overseas engagement and expansion of knowledge about the United States, its values and its people. Part of that shared endeavor stemmed from competition with Soviet-led communism, but it represented more than that: U.S. citizens, then and now, believe that they have things worth exporting and emulating, from ideas and forms of governance to art, music, scientific discoveries, high technology, and business know-how. This call for making a contribution to human betterment lay at the root of President Kennedy's inauguration of the Peace Corps and his outreach to Latin America. It was also intrinsic in his call for U.S. citizens themselves to "ask what [they] could do for [their] country." It also imbues the notion that history connotes progress and that progress, not stasis, is the norm in society.

Leader America—in the Mirror

What does national culture have to do with U.S. national intelligence, how it comes to be produced, what those products say, and how they are used? This author rejects the notion that nations have a national psyche (be it U.S., Somali, Cuban, or otherwise), but there are shared national traditions, histories, myths, legends, stories, lexicons, and images that have an appreciable effect on what becomes national intelligence. The United States is certainly no exception to this phenomenon. It is universal. "Americans [like most, if not all, others] formed their habits of government by solving a set of problems specific to their circumstances. And we know that habits often outlast the circumstances that justified them... ."[184] This observation also accounts for national culture as we understand it and employ it here.

---

182 See Samuel P. Huntington, Who Are We: The Challenges to America's National Identity (New York:
Simon and Schuster, 2004), and Arthur M. Schlesinger, Jr., The Disuniting of America: Reflections on a Multicultural Society (New York: Whittle, 1991, reprinted Norton, 1998).

183 Dean Acheson, Present at the Creation: My Years in the State Department (New York: W.W. Norton and Co., 1969).

184 Eric Rauchway, Blessed Among Nations: How the World Made America (New York: Hill & Wang, 2006), 5.

For most of its 232 years of independence, U.S. leaders and its informed public have considered the country to be indispensable[185] for global human freedom and progress. The concept of U.S. "exceptionalism" has been long debated, but it has two key elements: not only is the United States deemed, by its proponents, to be special; the U.S. is held up to be *the* exception when its behavior is compared to the traditional behavior of states, based on the unique quality, values, and resilience of its democracy. From the time of the Revolution in 1776, many U.S. citizens have deemed their country divinely inspired to lead the world as the enduring, primary protector and promulgator of freedom, peace, justice, and equality of opportunity.

Part of this legacy has been an element of evangelizing in U.S. foreign policy. From Governor John Winthrop in 1630 to Thomas Paine (in *Common Sense* in the mid-18th century) and to Ronald Reagan in the 1980s, then to neo-Wilsonian President George W. Bush today, America has been depicted, and has seen itself, as the "city on the hill," in essence as an exceptionally empowered beacon of hope and promise for all mankind.[186] This shared belief seems to justify the U.S. right to intervene in other countries in order to promote universal values through expanding the reach of liberty and democracy to others who are oppressed. U.S. citizens have long believed—and have been told by their elected leaders—that it is the United States which has set the norms and standards of international behavior, self-sacrifice, and furtherance of the highest human values and aspirations.[187] This, added to the sense of exceptionalism, makes for an unrelenting claim to universalism, something Samuel Huntington points to as a cause of global dissension between "the West and the rest."[188] America's wars have never been for territorial aggrandizement, so we are given to believe, but rather have been waged to "make the world safe for democracy" and "to end all

---

185 Former U.S. Secretary of State Madeleine Albright repeatedly called the United States "indispensable."

186 Paine envisaged that "...we [American colonists] have it in our power to begin the world over again...," quoted from A. James Reichley, Religion in American Public Life (Washington, DC: Brookings, 62.) For a fresh, well-argued characterization of contemporary American nationalism, see Anatol Lieven, America Right or Wrong: An Anatomy of American Nationalism (Oxford: Oxford University Press, 2004). An even more recent book theorizes that much of America's failure in world affairs owes to a misguided missionizing rooted in unique visions of exceptionalism. See Stefan Halper and Jonathan Clarke, The Silence of the Rational Center: Why American Foreign Policy is Failing (New York: Basic Books, 2007), and a critical review by Josef Joffe, "The Big Idea," Washington Post Book World, 8 April 2007, 5.

187 It is in their competing claims to be the herald of universal human rights, vanguard for improving the world, and birthplace of modern democracy that America and France (each citing its own democratizing revolution in the 18th century) are so much alike, even as they contend in a seemingly eternal quarrel over many issues.

188 Samuel P. Huntington, The Clash of Civilizations: The Remaking of World Order (New York: Simon & Schuster, 1996), 66f.

wars."[189] Moreover, U.S. citizens have never suffered a loss of territory or sovereignty from attacks on their homeland, notwithstanding Pearl Harbor or the 11 September 2001 terrorist assaults.

One must hasten to add, however, that even listing a number of widely-held views and traits common to many U.S. citizens now and in earlier generations, by no means are any of these views universally subscribed to. *There is no single U.S. point of view or unified stance on any issue, be it Iraq, abortion, the environment, or health care.* There is no single national mindset. Thus, while many remind us that the United States began as and remains predominantly Anglo-Saxon in its inheritance, that generalization decreases in validity with each passing year and with each wave of new immigrants, primarily from the South. What is important to note, in this context, is not just that so many generations have heard and felt the impact of lofty claims of U.S. altruism and self-sacrifice, but, in this author's experience, few perceive such pronouncements and "national beliefs" to be chauvinistic or self-serving. Those politicians, scholars, and commentators who dare to question the validity of this image of a self-giving country run the risk of being accused of "un-American, unpatriotic" behavior.

To get a sense of the ongoing political and cultural debates in the United States, one must read Michael Scheuer, Robert Kagan, or Clyde Prestowitz.[190] A value-laden debate swirls around U.S. intelligence culture and its output, a debate often waged by its own retired or dissenting cadre. Despite all its deserved plaudits, U.S. national intelligence has been the locus for decades of missing or mistaken judgments about how we might best interact with the rest of the world's countries.

Is there a lasting effect on U.S. national intelligence capabilities and evolutionary tendencies from this culture of self-criticism? The work of authors cited in the next section suggests the answer is "yes."

Roots of the Prevailing Intelligence Culture in the United States

Anatol Lieven reminds us of the overwhelming U.S. security and intelligence mindsets rooted in the experience of the 1945-1989 Cold War. It was then that Americans developed or matured "a certain innate tendency to see the

---

189 These comments are attributed to Woodrow Wilson who, in calling for a declaration of war in 1917, said: "The world must be made safe for democracy....We have no selfish ends to serve. We desire no conquest, no dominion." "Address to the Congress Asking for Declaration of War," 2 April 1917. (Reprinted in John A. Vasquez, Classics of International Relations, 3rd ed. (Upper Saddle River, New Jersey: Prentice Hall, 1996), 38.

190 See Robert Kagan, Of Paradise and Power (New York: Knopf, 2003) and Dangerous Nation (New York: Knopf, 2006); Michael Scheuer, Imperial Hubris: Why the West is Losing the War on Terror (Dulles, VA: Potomac Books, 2005); and Clyde Prestowitz, Rogue Nation: American Unilateralism and the Failure of Good Intentions (New York: Basic Books, 2004).

world as characterized by opposition and actual or potential hostility between states, rather than by a potential for cooperation...."[191] This Hobbesian worldview typifies the attitudes, priorities, and pre-occupations of U.S. national intelligence.[192] **The focus of U.S. national intelligence is on threats; its primary purpose, consumers, and priorities lie in the fields of national defense and, most recently post-9/11, in homeland security.** Lieven goes on to fault this pre-occupation with threats for blinding U.S. citizens not only to many opportunities for international cooperation but also to new threats which lie outside the scope of traditional "realist" categories, with global warming a prime example.[193]

Another commentator finds this same Cold War imprint on U.S. policies and attitudes equally compelling and points to three overarching, influential characteristics of that culture-shaping U.S.-Soviet conflict. It was a political and a military confrontation and competition, it was protracted, and it was global. Perhaps even more importantly, many of the U.S. decision-makers of today were in their formative years during the Cold War and bear its perceptual earmarks.[194] Clearly, we still live in the detritus of that Cold War, awaiting, as Richard Haass has pointed out, an appropriate name for the era now dawning.[195]

One additional cultural pattern that might be discerned is the overwhelming association of intelligence with foreign issues, rather than internal security, except for the memorable "McCarthy Era" of the early Cold War years. In that light, former UN Undersecretary-General Brian Urquhart writes angrily of the dichotomy between the Bush Administration's international behavior, especially going into and occupying Iraq, and the historic U.S. legacy of creative leadership in fostering the "concept and the substance of international law."[196] His complaint is that America has now turned its back on its own systemic creations designed to manage key elements of an otherwise anarchic world, even as the U.S. now exhibits unbecoming hypocrisy in flaunting some of the rules and

---

191   Lieven, America Right or Wrong: An Anatomy of American Nationalism (New York: Oxford University Press, 2004), vii.

192   For an incisive discussion of the phenomenon of threat in a national security context see Nobel Prize winner Thomas C. Schelling, The Strategy of Conflict (Cambridge, MA: Harvard University Press), 1960.

193   Lieven, vii. His concern has been addressed by a forthcoming National Intelligence Estimate that examines the security implications of global warming. See Mark Mazzetti, "Spy Chief Backs Study of Impact of Warming," New York Times, 12 May 2007. http://www.nytimes.com/2007/05/12/washington/12intel.html.

194   Donald M. Snow, National Security for a New Era (New York: Pearson Longman, 2007), 98-124.

195   See Richard N. Haass, "This Isn't Called the [Blank] Era for Nothing," The Washington Post (Outlook), 8 January 2006, B4.

196   Brian Urquhart, "The Outlaw World," New York Review of Books, 11 May 2006, 24.

organs it first had formulated. As we consider the ongoing transformation of U.S. intelligence, this "potent mix of ideals and self-interest" typifies U.S. "strategic culture."[197]

Sources of a Persistent U.S. National Intelligence Malaise

Americans see themselves as risk takers and innovators. Risk, however, entails a clear potential for failure. Failure in the contemporary conduct of national intelligence can have and has had enormous, negative consequences. In the first eight years of this new century, America has experienced two notable "failures" of national intelligence. If figuratively equated with sins, one (not anticipating or preventing 9/11) was of omission; the other, presuming to know that Saddam Hussein "still had" weapons of mass destruction in hand, was of commission. In both cases, untold costs and consequences have ensued, and America is a much more anxious, divided, and discomfited society as a result.

In the aftermath of those two seminal cases, expectations and demands directed at the massive, expensive Intelligence Community have only grown. Congressional legislation has become a prime mover in directing the executive branch's Intelligence Community in terms of its organization and regulation, and even what it will collect and analyze. Despite the long and rather spotty record of carrying out its oversight functions, the U.S. Congress is now a demanding player in the conduct of U.S. intelligence in all its disciplines and domains.[198]

U.S. citizens may claim to embrace risk when it comes to business and entrepreneurship, not to mention rock climbing and sky-diving, but its political decision-makers have no appetite for surprise. Instead, they expect simple (black and white), straightforward analysis with which to shape decisions, even though the world's complexity and potential intelligence targeting by adversaries appear to have increased. Analysts, on the other hand, generally see the world and its trends, states, and leaders in shades of gray. They insist that policy-maker concerns and questions demand nuanced, complicated responses. They often

---

197 Jennifer E. Sims, "Understanding Ourselves," Transforming U.S. Intelligence, Jennifer E. Sims and Burton Gerber, eds. (Washington, DC: Georgetown University Press, 2005), 36.

198 See Anne Miles, The Creation of the National Imagery and Mapping Agency: Congress's Role as Overseer, and Kevin E. Wirth, The Coast Guard Intelligence Program Enters the Intelligence Community, Occasional Papers 9 and 16 (Washington, DC: National Defense Intelligence College, 2002 and 2007); both available at http://www.ndic.edu. Also see Frank Smist, Jr., Congress Oversees the United States Intelligence Community, 1947-1989 (Knoxville: The University of Tennessee Press, 1990).

believe, as analysts, that their insights are discounted when it comes to imparting cultural, political, and societal information—and with some reason.[199]

U.S. intelligence—despite the wisdom of former National Intelligence Council Chairman Joseph Nye, who cautioned that national intelligence systems need to focus more on unfathomable mysteries than on unearthing secrets [200]—is caught up in a sea of rising expectations. One can fail in business, declare bankruptcy, and start over in the United States. It is an everyday occurrence. No such possibilities exist for U.S. national intelligence and its thousands of practitioners. There is neither an acceptable excuse nor place to hide in the aftermath of an "intelligence failure."

U.S. citizens tend to believe that they are quite intelligent and, thus, that they can prosper in a world that is increasingly knowledge-based and -driven. They even pair the adjective "smart" with technology—smart weapons, smart bombs, smart cards—and with policy ideas, such as the notion that one can devise "smart" (meaning specifically targeted) economic "sanctions." Above all, citizens want their government and the intelligence apparatus that helps inform its policies to be smart and act smartly. Many of the Intelligence Community's most vocal critics clearly consider themselves smarter than those tasked with creating national intelligence. Thus, as Cynthia Grabo and many others have lamented, 20-20 hindsight tends to dominate after a crisis has ensued and others begin plowing through the intelligence reports or information items received.[201] U.S. intelligence analysts (and the policy-makers they serve) have been inattentive to the debilitating ability of our targets and adversaries, using denial and deception, to "outsmart" us. Such has proved to be the case in both the 9/11 episode and in the declared U.S. motives for going to war against Iraq.

A further complication for the world of national intelligence in the United States is the proliferation of information sources and commentators. As part of the phenomenon called the "CNN factor," analysts have lost to television and other media any monopoly on delivering news, current information, and

---

[199] The author was personally involved in cases such as the fall of the Shah (1979), the breakup of former Yugoslavia (1990), Milosevic's will to resist (1999), and the 2003 U.S. invasion of Iraq, all of which are examples of the mismatch between analyst and policy-maker expectations.

[200] Joseph S. Nye, Jr. "Peering into the Future," Foreign Affairs, Vol. 73, No. 4 (July/August 1994), 82-93.

[201] "Even when the indications were not very good, or highly contradictory, or the adversary's course of action was truly illogical, investigations or other critiques usually managed to make much of the various fragments of information which were given inadequate attention when they came in or which pointed to the possibility that the adversary would take the course of action which he actually did." Cynthia Grabo, Anticipating Surprise: Analysis for Strategic Warning (Washington, DC: Joint Military Intelligence College, 2002 (http://www.ndic.edu/press/5671.htm) and Lanham, Maryland: University Press of America, 2004), 158.

even expert insights. Talking heads and instant commentators dominate the airwaves; all-news, all-the-time broadcasting has become a fundamental component of life in the U.S. However, there is little, if any, evidence that Americans know or care more about the rest of the world than in years past.[202] Rather, the evidence tends to point to the contrary, and we remain fixated on ourselves.

Notwithstanding the Intelligence Community's (particularly by analysts in the Department of State) warning against the U.S. invasion of Iraq, which was ignored by the most senior policy-makers,[203] a recent example of self-referencing interpretation of information was the U.S. media's failure to exercise its traditional investigative role in reporting and critiquing U.S. intentions, plans, and policies vis-a-vis Iraq in 2002 and 2003. The fourth estate, a key node in the complex system of U.S. political checks and balances, failed utterly to be an independent, convincing voice examining the prospects and varying rationale for U.S. intervention in Iraq and its aftermath.[204]

U.S. Intelligence Culture: Privacy, Openness, Speed, and the Primacy of Collection and Technology

The U.S. Intelligence Community, with its 16 agencies, earns a dual label—colossal and expensive. This massive enterprise contradicts some standard national values. The Community demands and defends secrecy inside of what its citizens hold to be the most liberal, open society on earth. The "secret order" of intelligence now includes two to three million individuals who hold

---

202   One recent indicator pointing in this direction is the Pew Global Attitudes Survey of 2006 which found that, on the controversial issue of U.S. prisoner abuse at Abu Graib, 98 per cent of Germans surveyed were aware of the issue but only 76 percent of Americans. Pew goes on to state its overall finding: "For the most part, Americans are significantly less aware of events and issues than are the publics in Germany and other major industrialized countries." Poll Global Attitudes Project, 13 June 2006, *http://pewglobal.org/reports/display.php?-ReportID=252*, accessed 10 April 2007. American favorable opinion toward the United Nations fell from 77 percent in 2001 to 51 percent in the 2006 poll.

203   Report of the Select Committee on Intelligence on Prewar Intelligence Assessments about Postwar Iraq (Washington, DC: U.S. Senate), 110th Cong. 1st Sess., 25 May 2007, available at *http://www.intelligence.senate.gov/prewar.pdf*. Paul Pillar, "Inside Track: Sometimes the CIA is Right," The National Interest Online, 6 June 2007, *http://www.nationalinterest.org/Article.aspx?id=14564*, recounts how this warning was ignored.

204   Nowhere is this fact laid out more clearly or more convincingly than in "Now They Tell Us," the critical review essay by Michael Massing in which, among others, he concluded: "In the period before the [Iraq] war, US journalists were far too reliant on sources sympathetic to the administration. Those with dissenting views—and there were more than a few—were shut out... the coverage was highly deferential to the White House....As journalists rush to chronicle the administration's failings on Iraq, they should pay some attention to their own." While the New York Times comes in for Massing's greatest criticism, two Knight-Ridder national security reporters are applauded for seriously scrutinizing administration claims and consulting working-level sources involved in the intelligence analysis being carried out, or sometimes being stifled. The New York Review of Books, 51, no. 3 (26 February 2004), 43.

government security clearances,[205] even as Washington itself is awash in intelligence leaks. Nonetheless, the idea that secrecy is required to protect America's openness from outside harm, and that the public, while entitled to know most of what its government is doing, does not and should not have access to everything, is not widely contested.

Transparency, in the form of media-covered Congressional hearings, press conferences, government documents, websites, and more, characterize the U.S. approach to openness. Demands for sunshine laws and public access to the legislative process have ushered in the era of C-Span coverage of countless hours of Congressional debate and more. On the other hand, protection of intellectual property, copyrights, patents, trade secrets, proprietary formulas and techniques, and even company logos as protected trademarks are also intrinsic to U.S. citizens' understanding that some things and some information require and deserve protection. Indeed, one could make the argument that there is no bigger, better kept secret in America than the formula for Coca Cola syrup, a trade secret guarded as zealously as U.S. war plans.[206]

Privacy remains a fundamental right in the United States, one closely guarded in the face of government intrusion brought on by resort to "warrantless wiretaps" under the USA PATRIOT Act. To assist in realizing this right, the U.S. has enacted both privacy and freedom of information laws to afford citizens access to internal government data—subject to security review for redaction or selective non-release. But the default position of the government now is to declassify virtually all information not clearly requiring continuing national security protection. When the PATRIOT Act and some of the more intrusive anti-terrorism measures were enacted or disclosed, many citizens of the U.S. recoiled in anger and suspicion. Some voiced the view that, if America's security required it and a person had nothing to hide, no harm was done. Many others were adamant that government "snooping" without warrants and without evident probable cause was impermissible and a violation of their most basic civil and legal rights. Despite these pressures and conflicting attitudes, the forced marriage in the United States between maximum govern-

---

205   Meena Thiruvengadam, "Security Clearance a Golden Ticket," *http://www.clearance-jobs.com/index.php?action=article&num=16*, accessed 4 June 2007.

206   In a recent case, a Coca Cola employee offered insider information about that substance to a rival beverage manufacturer, was apprehended, and sentenced to eight years imprisonment—a rarity for those who leak U.S. intelligence information. A PepsiCo employee reported the breach to Coca Cola security, further testimony of the allegiance to or systemic dependence on the sanctity of industrial secrets. See Chico Harlan, "Trade secret plot pulls Coke, Pepsi together," Pittsburgh Post-Gazette, 7 July 2006. *http://www.post-gazette.com/pg/06188/704045-28.stm.*

mental openness and security for critical national information and intelligence holdings remains intact, even if continuously challenged.[207]

Just as defining a unitary U.S. culture proves elusive, that same lack of an over-arching culture typifies the U.S. Intelligence Community. Many structures and institutional devices, such as the Community-validated National Intelligence Strategy,[208] seek to promote a common effort, but cultural barriers persist and are formidable. There are not only 16 separate agency cultures but also several competing, contending cultures within most agencies. In an attempt to break up, or through, the existing cultures, mindsets, and group-dictated habits and norms, reformers encounter the daunting challenge of creating a Community-wide set of standards and methodologies, the seminal task of the new Director of National Intelligence (DNI) and his ever-growing staff.

By way of illustration, intelligence collectors zealously protect sources and apply need-to-know restrictions on information distribution, and they are quite distrustful of foreign (and at times even their own U.S. analytical) counterparts. Analysts, on the other hand, generally want more information more widely shared, are eager to test their ideas and judgments with others outside their own circle (given the permission and time to do so), and yearn for the opportunity to reflect in order to reach informed analytical judgments and interpretations. All-source analysts clamor for all of the information they can get their hands on, tasked as they are to make sense of and anticipate events in a situation of perennial uncertainty. Each of these sub-cultures, moreover, tends to perpetuate itself by educating and training its own progeny and its recruits into the existing agency culture, its norms, methods, and taboos, thus perpetuating cultural gaps and biases.

One key ingredient of the national intelligence culture, in keeping with the infatuation of many citizens with speed and self-service, is "intelligence on demand." Those who collect intelligence are charged with finding secure ways with which to make more of what they collect and process available to more and more users/consumers—and rapidly. This circle of users now includes: all ranks and operators in the military (many of whom have minimal, if any, security clearances); state and local police, and other "first responders"; and now the body of intelligence professionals and policy- and decision-makers in a growing federal community of users, most recently encompassing thousands more homeland security and defense personnel.

---

207   CIA Director General Michael Hayden made this point succinctly: "We [U.S. intelligence] are a powerful, secret organization inside of a political culture that only distrusts two things: power and secrecy." C-Span Q&A Podcasts with Brian Lamb, 15 April 2007. http://www.q-and-a.org/Transcript/?ProgramID=1123, accessed 17 April 2007.

208   See the National Intelligence Strategy published in 2005 at http://www.dni.gov/publications/NISOctober2005.pdf.

Intelligence in the United States has long been dominated, in terms of bureaucratic power and spending priorities, by those who collect—rather than analyze—intelligence. And, with the collectors first among equals, technology has long been the major preoccupation of the collection disciplines, and the two together the preferred avenue for seeking solutions to intelligence problems. Technology, however, can create vulnerabilities at the same time as it creates new strengths. Moreover, just as conventional armies and tactics are ill-suited for effective counter-insurgency operations, technically acquired intelligence is not particularly well-suited for discovering well-concealed plots or ferreting out terrorists who are astutely aware of intelligence collection capabilities and keen to insure their operational and information security. Today's terrorists remain the ultimate conundrum for all existing collection disciplines, even as we acknowledge that "it takes a network to defeat a network."[209]

A number of U.S. warfare and terrorism experts have observed over the past 40 years that the U.S. defense and intelligence establishments are poorly matched to deal with highly mobile, concealed, networked practitioners of Fourth Generation Warfare. Emphasis on massing firepower, employing high technology tools, and counting bodies is not the solution.[210] Others, of course, fully recognize the nature of the challenge of transnational terrorism. In his confirmation hearing as Director of CIA, General Michael Hayden made it clear that "[T]his is a long war, and it's not just going to be won with heat, blast and fragmentation. It is fundamentally a war of ideas."[211] At the same time, no one has ready answers to compensate for the apparent weakness of technical

---

209 While this observation may have various origins, I take it from the comments of Dr. Markus Ederer, former chief of analysis of the German Federal Intelligence Service (BND), made during the "New Frontiers" international intelligence analysis symposium organized by the Global Futures Project and held in Rome, Italy, April 2004. See also the work of Rob Johnston, Analytic Culture in the U.S. Intelligence Community: An Ethnographic Study (Washington, DC: Center for the Study of Intelligence, 2005), which explores the penchant of U.S. intelligence and U.S. culture for individualism, which works against achieving networked teams of analysts and others to work against networked adversaries.

210 See, among others, Thomas X. Hammes, The Sling and the Stone (St Paul, MN: Zenith, 2004), and Brian M. Jenkins, The Unchangeable War, RAND Publication RM-6278-2-ARPA, November 1970 (RAND Corporation: Santa Monica, CA, 1970). Jenkins, writing about Vietnam, notes: "Enemy soldiers continue to die at a greater rate than our own, but we do not know how many enemy soldiers must die before the enemy's will cracks or his army begins to disintegrate...more troubling than our apparent failures...is our inability to learn and apply lessons from these failures...[by those] who believe that 'victory' ...could have been or still can be accomplished with more—either more troops, more time, or more latitude in the application of our military power" (emphases in original), 2. Hammes, referring to Iraq and contemporary conflicts, faults Joint Vision 2010 for not confronting the "how" of achieving "information dominance"—the "foundation of the vision," p. 6. Neither commentator offers novel or useful ideas on improving intelligence in support of their military proposals and critiques.

211 Hearing of the Senate Select Committee on Intelligence, Room 216, Hart Senate Office Building, http://www.dni.ic.gov/dni/ssecihearingmorningsession051806.pdf, accessed 12 April 2007.

and human intelligence collection activities against such "hit, run, and hide" targets which exploit global telecommunications, the Internet, and other "dual-use" facets of globalization.

Ever advancing, more sophisticated technology involves costly, time-consuming research and development, production, testing and evaluation before it becomes operational. A key concern, among both policy and intelligence officials, is the expense and delays incurred in development of new satellites and national technical means of intelligence collection. That said, this author has observed a tendency among policy consumers who are eager to view the products of such collection firsthand and to analyze the data personally. Also troublesome is the occasional bias toward a particular intelligence collection discipline among analysts who ply their trade within a given U.S. national intelligence collection agency. There is ample, if anecdotal, evidence that "all-source" analysts working in an agency where HUMINT dominates the agenda, for example, tend to place greater value and focus on that discipline in their analyses than on others; a similar observation holds for SIGINT and imagery-focused personnel.[212]

National Exceptionalism and Intelligence Sources

One facet of U.S. national culture that remains even after the Cold War is the appeal or magnetism of the country for some who live abroad. This phenomenon has direct intelligence relevance, as it did throughout the Cold War. That is, not only are millions of individuals eager to migrate to America's shores in search of opportunities and a better, freer life, but in addition some possess the motivation and courage to desert their foreign intelligence organizations, military hierarchies, or scientific institutes to defect to the United States. Such defectors, while always subject to deception suspicions, have no doubt brought valuable, critical insights and information with them. While their motivations vary, those who do so most wholeheartedly tend to act primarily for ideological and idealistic reasons. In his historical sketches of post-World War II Soviet intelligence defectors, one author notes that the trend of defection explanations saw a rise in those persons who deserted the USSR based on an impulse that was "entirely ideological, a moral revulsion against Communism because of the

---

212 The author and colleagues observed this intermittently in national intelligence production debates among analysts and in analytic output from CIA counterparts responsible for the former National Intelligence Daily (NID). A contrary allegation is also leveled, at times, at all-source analysts in the Department of State's Bureau of Intelligence and Research (INR)—that they erred in favor of diplomatic reporting and are more given to analytical optimism in seeing diplomatic opportunities than are other U.S. intelligence analysts. Having worked in INR all-source analysis for 27 years, this author was more often accused by counterparts in State Department regional and functional bureaus of being unduly pessimistic.

corruption, deceit and terror in which it was rooted."[213] This stream of defectors can be expected to continue so long as they remain confident of being positively received, resettled, and given new identities or "lives."[214]

U.S. Intelligence, Know Thyself

Shortly before his death, eminent U.S. historian Arthur Schlesinger reminded his fellow countrymen that "[A] nation needs to know its own history [and] a nation denied a conception of its past will be disabled in dealing with its present and its future."[215] Historical remnants of national culture, many Americans seem to believe, are too expensive to retain—or it retards economic growth and modernization. The U.S. obsession with the new and the youthful is hard to overlook. Not surprisingly, then, astute awareness of history (both among intelligence analysts and policy-makers) and the application of that awareness remains a critical cultural failing.[216] A glaring recent case in point was ignorance (either not knowing or purposefully glossing over) the British experience in Iraq in 1917.[217]

Given the enduring pre-eminence of collection over analysis, notwithstanding repeated calls to rebalance their relationship, the language of "tradecraft" has encroached on the work of analysis, claiming to offer a more scientific way to engage in the cognitive approach to analysis.[218] However, expertise applied by faceless analysts is often not trusted. Self-service analysis and raw intelligence interpretation by those who are not subject matter experts are no doubt widespread across the world. In the U.S., senior veterans of government have cautioned both the Intelligence Community and their own policy-level successors against this very phenomenon.[219]

---

213 Gordon Brook-Shepherd, The Stone Birds: Soviet Postwar Defectors (New York: Weidenfeld & Nicolson, 1989), xi-xiii. Also see Pete Earley's book on recent Russian defector Sergei Tretyakov, Comrade J: The Untold Secrets of Russia's Master Spy in America after the End of the Cold War (New York: Putnam, 2008).

214 To find specifics on a range of such defectors, see The Cold War Project, link to Defectors, at http://www.videofact.com/english/defectors_en.html, accessed 4 June 2007.

215 Arthur Schlesinger, Jr. "History and National Stupidity," The New York Review of Books, 27 April 2006, 14.

216 A seminal work addressing this theme in intelligence terms is Ernest R. May and Richard E. Neustadt, Thinking In Time: The Uses of History for Decision-Makers (New York: Free Press, 1988).

217 See Robert Fisk, "Iraq, 1917," The Independent (UK), 17 June 2004, http://www.informationclearinghouse.info/article6337.htm, accessed 4 June 2007.

218 See the seminal work of Richards J. Heuer, Jr., Psychology of Intelligence Analysis (Washington, DC: Center for the Study of Intelligence, 1999), and the recent work of David T. Moore, Critical Thinking and Intelligence Analysis, Occasional Paper 14 (Washington, DC: Joint Military Intelligence College, 2006).

219 Strobe Talbott, as he departed as U.S. Deputy Secretary of State, made this his main theme in meeting with the Bureau of Intelligence and Research (INR) in December 2000. Colin Powell, as Secretary of State, told INR's analytic workforce that the added value for him lay first of all in the judgments we would and did provide.

Competition and Collaboration

Competition is a traditional hallmark of the makeup and conduct of U.S. public life. It applies in the commercial marketplace and in the marketplace of ideas and opinions. Protection of intellectual property is a mainstay of U.S. foreign and trade policy, but it is a major hindrance to collaboration in U.S. intelligence. While businesses rightly protect their proprietary trade secrets, too many in the U.S. intelligence culture remain unwilling to make their collected secrets available even across the trusted community of intelligence analysts and consumers whose work relies on such access.

This dysfunctional approach to collection and product sharing, as well as in collaborative analysis, has long been a feature of U.S. national intelligence, oftentimes in ways not supportive of policy-makers. The U.S. record of cultures in competition and a disjointed delivery of intelligence reach back to Pearl Harbor, to assessments of Soviet missile strengths, to gauging the progress of the Vietnam War, and much more. The same was again painfully in evidence in both the 9/11 and Iraq invasion episodes, to the point where the un-met demand for collaborative (and therefore competitive) analysis became recognized in law.[220] The lesson the U.S. allegedly learned, unlike that of the British in their institution of the Joint Intelligence Committee and their focus on generating consensus analysis, was that groupthink and institutional bias were the biggest challenges to intelligence for national security policymaking.

We continue the quest for the golden mean, one which will have the U.S. intelligence apparatus fall victim neither to prevailing groupthink nor to immutable mindsets. By the same token, policy cannot effectively make use of analysis which presents a broad range of disparate and conflicting views if intelligence is to be an effective instrument for informing—not forming—U.S. national security strategy and foreign policies. For now, it seems the emphasis is back on competitive analysis and overlapping collection systems, even as the Office of the DNI works to forge more collaboration and a greater sense among the numerous participants of being and acting as a community.

---

220   The most recent DNI "100-Day Plan for INTEGRATION and COLLABORATION" [all caps in original], issued April 2007, again focuses on moving toward an intelligence "culture of collaboration" and of "responsibility to provide" (a semantic renovation from earlier 9/11 Commission terminology of moving from "need to know" to "need to share"). Patterned after the U.S. military's emphasis on "jointness," the ambitious plan seeks to break down the U.S. Intelligence Community's ingrained proprietary attitude of "information collected is information owned," even as demands for sources and methods protection continue as insurmountable hurdles to such a revolutionary cultural shift. The Intelligence Reform and Terrorism Prevention Act of 2004 reads, in part, "[T]he Director of National Intelligence shall...ensure that the elements of the intelligence community regularly conduct competitive analysis of analytic products...." (SEC. 102A (h) Analysis (1) (C), 7 December 2004.

In sum, the U.S. national intelligence culture reflects many facets of U.S. national culture and most assuredly the overwhelming emphases of U.S. strategic culture. That is to say, it focuses on threats, is seeking to better cope with burgeoning global and transnational phenomena, and remains challenged by the need to ensure "global coverage" for a global superpower, even as it concentrates resources and attention on the most pressing current issues and conflicts. A fear, as always, is that the huge but dispersed U.S. national intelligence community and cultures will not be astute, agile, or observant enough to see strategic and lesser problems in gestation before they confront us head-on. Decision makers in government will continue to demand a "no surprises" capability from intelligence, even as they and those in the Community itself realize that such an expectation is, in fact, "mission impossible."

About the Author

Dr. Bowman H. Miller teaches at the National Defense Intelligence College in Washington, D.C. Before joining the NDIC faculty in August 2005, he served for 27 years in the U.S. Department of State, including in the Bureau of Intelligence and Research (INR). As a Senior Executive, he was Director of the Office of Analysis for Europe. Prior to his State Department career, Dr. Miller was a U.S. Air Force officer. His academic background includes study at the University of Iowa and at Cornell, assignment as a Fulbright Scholar at the Eberhard-Karls University in Tuebingen, Germany, with completion of his formal education at Georgetown University where he received his doctorate in 1983. His dissertation analyzed the language factor and revolutionary/terrorist writings of the German Red Army Faction (aka Baader-Meinhof Group). His research interests include modern European history and contemporary European and trans-Atlantic affairs; Germany in all its aspects; terrorism and threat analysis; all-source foreign affairs analysis; cognitive barriers to analysis; the spectrum of conflict from ethnic disputes to global trends; and manipulation of language in politics and diplomacy. He serves on the Academic Advisory Council of the American Institute for Contemporary German Studies and has served on the editorial board of *International Studies Perspectives*. In 2005, he was awarded the German Officer's Cross of the Order of Merit (*Bundesverdienstkreuz*). Contact: *Bowman.Miller@dia.mil*.

ACKNOWLEDGMENTS

Russell G. Swenson and **Susana C. Lemozy,** as co-editors of this book, greatly appreciate the dedication of all the authors whose work appears here. Each author contributed a thoughtful essay that allowed the editors to better develop the theme. They also exhibited exquisite patience and understanding through multiple drafts and a long gestation. We also recognize the good will and professional perspective of the seasoned intellectuals Marco Cepik of Brazil and Jorge Serrano of Peru. For their linguistic skill and attention to detail, we also acknowledge the assistance of Frank Marcio de Oliveira and Hugo Alberto Lazar of Brazil, as well as of William Spracher, editor with the National Defense Intelligence College. The editors sincerely appreciate the continuing support of officials, educational colleagues, and students of the NDIC in the U.S. and of Argentina's *Instituto de Inteligencia de las Fuerzas Armadas.* Their continued support will ensure that both institutions remain seedbeds for an ever more mature understanding of intelligence.